The Treasure Within

Spiritual Channelings
from the mystic beyond

Written & illustrated
by Sana Mirza
Edited by Tania Chick

The Treasure Within

First edition

Copyright © 2023 Sana Mirza

Illustrations © 2023 Sana Mirza

All Rights Reserved

No part of this publication may be reproduced without written permission from the author except for the use of brief quotations in a social media post, review or article.

ISBN: 9798870424583

Published by Flourishing Goddess, London

fallriseflourish.com

*To my guide, Shaykh Hisham Kabanni,
for allowing me to embrace the journey
of submitting to the Higher Will.*

Contents

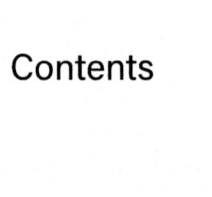

I The Wound   1

II The Entering   61

III The Light   116

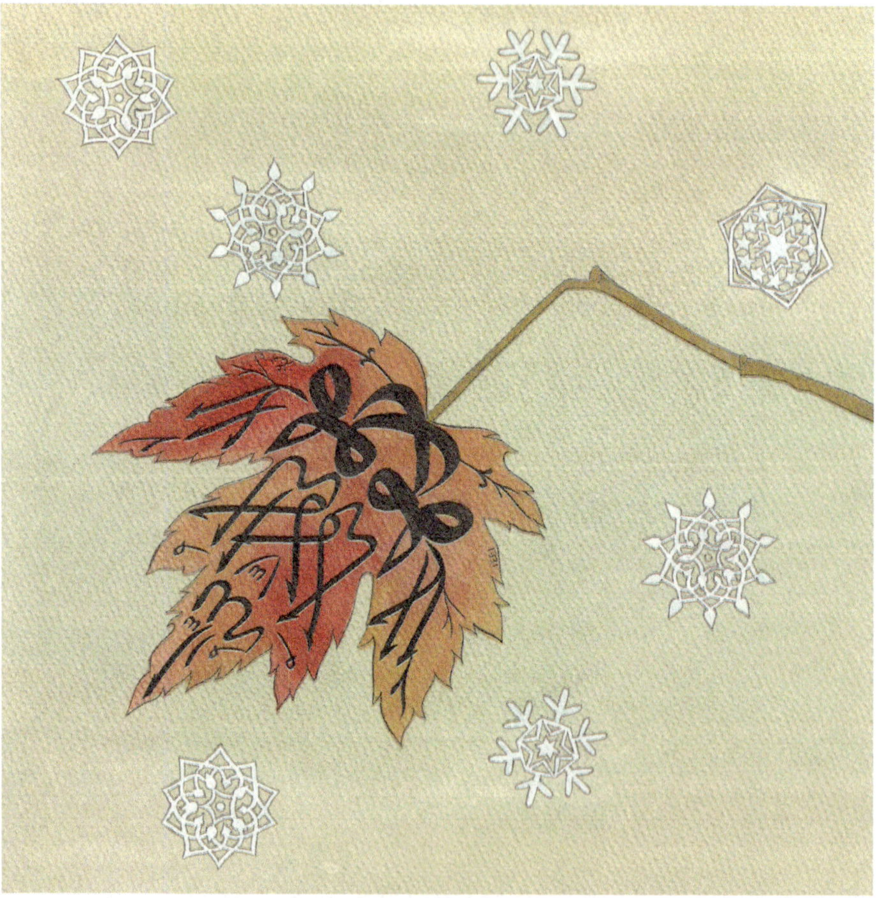

The Wound

*"Your treasure at the end
of the tunnel awaits you."*

Look through the magical eyes of infinity and all will work out in your favor. There is a grand plan at play. Trust that. You are always being asked to align with that higher will with your own free will. All is a training ground to get you to that point of mastering peace and moving towards your highest destiny. Never let the ego limit you on that. You are most capable and powerful as you align with God's Will to carry you.

- **4.14.23**

Release the stories and the heaviness attached to 3D situations and embrace the cosmic flow of manifestation always trying to reach you. To that open heart that truly knows and believes that God is carrying you in every moment no matter what. Focus on your soul's well-being and all will ultimately be of service to you. To raise you up into that ultimate phoenix of balance that has truly risen from the 3 dimensional and embraced the soul realm of grace, wonder and mystery. In the most mundane practical scenarios, you will be carried by an invisible power and protection.

- **3.31.23**

Ultimately, we are all here to awaken and how that plays out will look different for everyone. We cannot judge by earthly rules, for that only leads to logical brain induced convoluted dead ends. Even a delay in something is meant to be a blessing. Trust that, for you do not have the God's Eyes to see. Trust God above all and you will see how the creation manifestation will work to show you God's presence in everything and everyone. All sent as a mercy ultimately.

- **3.28.23**

Embrace the impossible and the expansiveness of all possibilities in every moment and watch true faith and power take over your life in the most unexpectedly miraculous ways. Let go of judgment, negativity, cynicism and illusion in all ways and watch everything to always be rigged in your favor. Keep an open mind no matter what. You have only yet to do this in new and profound ways.

- **3.10.23**

All is well on the other side of dualistic perspective. See from the eyes of oneness that all is connected, and all is part of the bigger plan. Let it work for your utmost highest favor and all those involved. You chose to learn the highest evolution of your soul. Everyone is getting there in their own unique ways. Have compassion most of all. Everyone is a divine gift to catalyze that process into being one with the ocean. Do you not desire to be one with grace?

- **2.10.23**

Peace is within you no matter what storm is unfolding. God's grace, the infinite universe, will grant you all that you need in every given moment. Trust that you are always protected. Rise in heaven within, so you may see it manifest all around you, no matter what. You are a master of your own energy. Own up to your own self, first and foremost. As the pain body releases all that you are not, see the process of cleansing through as a gift to get you to your highest soul essence, which links you to all that is infinite more and more, higher and higher- on the staircase of ascension we go!

- **1.13.23**

Do you believe in the miracle of this time?

Your reality will mirror to you exactly what you believe. Be a portal for divine essence. Pure mirrors lead to the ultimate union from within that manifests out. It calls for you to expand your horizons. It pushes you to really see where you are limited. The powerful new beginning and identity it is pushing you to step into. It enhances your senses to fill in the void where necessary. Be one with your shadow and create beautiful change with it.

Self-criticism is not in your vocabulary anymore. As long as you persist in self-loathing, you will manifest scenarios that will apt that very perspective. Don't you see that it is a game of simply maintaining a high vibe at all costs? That is your purpose, but no other exists but yourself- love is priority. People who are narcissistic look at others way more than they do themselves. The ironic part is when you look at you, that creates real change. This is not selfish for you to do so. It is an act of great wisdom that changes the cosmic wheel of destiny in your favor.

Higher destiny resides in higher planes. Stay in the upper planes and you will see it too. What and where are you still hiding in the dark about? It's about to shine a light on it. Be prepared to let go of the veils more and more. Because your true essence needs to shine in all ways. Good and bad, this is all about integration at a very core human level. Embrace it with all its power that it brings. You are a true believer in God consciousness. Be one with it. You are one with it.

- **11.25.22**

All that exists is within you and connects you to all that exists beyond time. Remove the veil of your ego mind that thinks there is a certain direction but move into the space of going through all obstacles for the illusion that they really are. Be one with all that is and is for your highest good. And it will be depending on your own perception what it will become. Beware of what your aura and energy is attracting at all times. This is real mastery.

- **11.18.22**

Embrace your true self that will magnetize you in becoming your diamond crystalline self in human form. Surrender to the cosmic ethereal flow of love. What you seek is always seeking you. Is your mirror clear and open enough to see it? Or are you distracted by the illusion right of what you think you are. Are you pushed to keep an image of some sort? Perhaps you feel you are not cool enough. You have always been beautiful to me. You must see it for yourself. Become more of You and all will fall into place with what is meant for you. You will never fail if you transform into what makes you purely you. The moth is always attracted to pure light. And the light is pure- you.

- **11.11.22**

What you are experiencing in your reality are not random acts of selfishness. They are timed lessons that must be integrated for the safe survival of your whole being in the days to come. A not fully integrated shadow side will result in misfiring of energy in the wrong direction. Because your body was not made capable of holding the light as well as the darkness. What perceives to be evil to you is only but an illusion of a greater good. The temptation is the gateway to your higher destiny made manifest. For all that you seek is still what you are tempted with. And what you seek is what you need to integrate. To be a fully embodied light being you must be able to look at the darkness straight in the eye and not judge. For if you judge you are not aware that that very thing is in you that needs nurturing.

Blessed be you for all the work you have done thus far. Your eminence calls for your presence in the higher realms. Where you dwell in peace in the knowing that all is divinely orchestrated. Trust in this knowing please. For you are a divine sovereign being made manifest in a physical body. Keep doing the beautiful work you are doing. For God sees you in the day and night. In your light and in your darkness. Don't think they are separate for one is good the other is bad. Listen to the pangs of your body, for that is where the lessons still lie, strengthening you day by day. You have done so well in retaining this powerful universal energy. Don't be afraid. For you have become the lion that has become fully tamed. A paradox is this game, yes indeed. Embrace the mystery.

- **8.7.22**

The divine does not care what we show on the outside. As long as the subconscious runs, there are always going to be inhibitions that act as blocks to whatever we're trying to achieve. And so is beauty in the eyes of the beholder. It's up to us to see everything rigged in our favor. Life really is programmed that way to serve you for your highest good. The more you see this, the more you experience it. Openings may come in ways that you may not recognize. But surely enough if we're open, we will see the answers to our innermost desires right in front. Staring at us right in the face with a calm smile. Here I am, answering the call to your prayers. Are you open enough to really see or blinded by your own resistance? It takes a lifetime of ego training to become part of this flow. To realize everything is truly in perfection.

- **7.9.22**

Don't forget to protect your energy by vibing in the higher octaves of your soul being. That requires you to be free from your own negativity most of all. The energy of love is always infinitely available to us. Sometimes the portal opens clear and wide. Do you feel how it wants you to come in and lose yourself to its infinite grace? Capture it now in the consciousness of your being. The clear mirror awaits you, to realize your own God given potential in a human vessel, disguised as nothing but angelic you are.

- 4.6.22

The heart knows what the mind does not know. Those who truly hear and see beyond illusion maintain a state of higher vision for the becoming of this higher destiny to unfold. Don't be fooled by the tricks of the ego that put a limit on your experience. Trust me, I was in a deep dark hole once too, where I felt lost and confused and in a state of hopelessness and the resistance was unbearable. But the truth is that I was saved by the grace of God. And to this day, all I have to do is believe that God has saved me once and he sure will save me many times again. He has the power, regardless of what we find impossible. Expect the unexpected from him. Because truly those in the mercy of this grace, which we all are swimming in- it's really just a matter of seeing it beyond the limited frame of mind. You will be astonished at how good your reality really is and how beautifully each detail is rigged in your favor. Do you see it?!

- **2.28.22**

This becomes a journey of merging the two polarities, until there remains no contradiction within you as a human fully integrated. This is the secret of the magnet. The void that pulls you in, only to be exploded into a big giant light star, quite literally. How this happens, you may ask? Well, it's an alchemical intoxication that occurs within you that opens the gates of ecstasy so powerful it awakens your senses to the max only to plumage you back into normal reality to see the heart wrenching duality of the difference of both. How to rectify this you may ask? Well, it becomes a process of integrating this ecstasy slowly, slowly to create and regain balance. To be a container of this requires highly compressive capabilities like a stone made into diamond with extreme pressure of pain applied at first, only to become immune to everything thrown your way. This is the magic of dark and light integration.

You have become it all in human form only to face, fear, pain, guilt and other lower emotions as non-existent after that. You become a match to its energy, face it, then transmute it into gold. This is an ultimate dying to your own self, only to be reborn in complete surrender to your activated lightbody with all dark aspects fully integrated. Not spiritually bypassed or running on autopilot in a disorderly way behind the scenes but becoming a happy part of you that knows you can conquer all. Demons and angels live in harmony tamed by you is the new paradigm of the new earth, awakening us all to true oneness in human form. This the secret to becoming formless.

- **2.3.22**

The universe is on your side, so whatever you think and believe Will happen. For better or for worse, so be careful what you manifest. Your will is the creators will in this game. Step outside the matrix and keep the higher vision. This is where your divine Self steps in. Outside of fear and illusion and disturbing circumstances is a reality that is waiting for you to join in harmony with. Merge with that new earth (cosmic consciousness). It's waiting for you up there where your mind doesn't rule but your heart just knows.

Be Inn Love.

- **1.27.22**

God consciousness is hard to implement if you don't exactly know why the good and the bad are very intertwined in a cosmic interplay of divinely orchestrated positions for the highest good of all. In whatever way the play unfolds, the illusion of disguised chaos is actually in order with divine perfection. So blessed are those who start to really see this reality play out. And so you start to see how everything and everyone is acting as a conduit of God in so many ways. If we can perceive where the path is really headed, we start to see the wisdom in why it is happening the way it is. It's a beautiful place to get to this point of true peacefulness. Because- all in all- everything is rigged in your favor. You better believe that it is. And the more we believe that it is, the more our so-called bad experiences flip for us in a favorable way.

The mirror is always on you to flip the illusions/ distortions to reflect the infinite pure mirror that you are. The more you polish, the more you will reflect back to you all that is pure and nothing less. The essence of all spiritual paths is the cleaning of the inner You. Ultimately you will only see what you are. Make it pure, just like sand, that helps you truly see with a blank slate. Align with love and watch miracles unfold.

- **11.25.21**

*Y*ou are always a mirror to your surroundings until you clear that mirror that keeps you blind to what you really want. And that takes work on ourselves in every shadowy way. And when you reach a point where the mirror becomes clear enough for you to decipher what is fake from what is real. That journey of realizing and becoming better and better at that becomes the gift in and of itself. And all those people or experiences that lead you to that point of becoming a true mirror to yourself becomes the ultimate experience, where you value yourself so much more than you did before. There is a gift in every experience, good or bad. It still opens you to higher realities because ultimately everything is sent as a mercy and a knowing of yourself and God. Hu I Am in my purest state is what I want to attract and reset into that awareness every time you lose focus on the higher goal and your own legacy.

- 11.9.21

The spiritual can look like quite a maze sometimes, but with the right frequency of love, no matter what path or situation unfolds, you can experience it with the utmost heightened ability no matter what the outer circumstance. You choose the timeline you want to experience based on your level of consciousness and how much wisdom you want to extract from it. Seemingly untimely, everything truly is in divine time. To see that requires for us to open up our divine vision as well. And for us to open up to that divine vision requires us to let go of everything we think we know about anything and embrace the unknown in all ways.

I've seen this with the miracles that unexpectedly unfolded in my life to show me plenty of times that God was running the show, not me. All I had to do was align my vision to truly see that it was unfolding just as it should be. Do we really think that God would let us be in our own chaos? Never are we ever outside of this divine perfection. The sooner we realize this, the sooner we will be able to embrace *the all* that is working in our favor *at all* times. And let go of our preconceived notions of reality, because God certainly exists way beyond that, in the midst of what we label as impossible. Nothing is impossible for God. Only we label it so. Love will certainly guide us through all the seemingly real illusions and confusions. Love takes that heaviness away and carries us there like a magic carpet that has no strings attached. It just opens whenever you tap into its energy.

So be love whenever you can. It's as simple as that.

- 10.21.21

Your treasure at the end of the tunnel awaits you.

What has taken you so long to eliminate your doubts about this? Examine that and you will propel and excel forward. The timeline is for you to choose. But first you must learn some things. Honor that process of learning. What you discover in those learning experiences (aka- temporary rooms of self-acknowledgement) may surprise you. Walk out with ease when the time comes. For you will know when you are ready. The universe, in all ways, will align you for this. Take action in all ways possible to anchor this forthcoming/ homecoming. And destiny itself shall set you free.

Your breakthroughs, in karma especially, lie in continuously choosing the highest most neutral timeline for yourself. As the polarity that is one sided begins to break, your union will manifest more and more in the physical. Trust this knowing and clear all doubts. For the universe is on your side in all ways. And you know it. When the sun and moon come together, a cosmic collision happens and creation is born. Choose wisely what you would like to create with this third energy.

- **10.8.21**

It's about transcending the ego to rise higher than the collective drama and false masks of separation. Know that your reality will change once you've reached a level of mastery within yourself of acceptance, peacefulness, and calm. And all angelic help will be at your service. Resist the temptation to falter from this. For the key to your heaven solely lies within you. For our realities to shift from separation consciousness to unity consciousness, it is going to be about stepping up to the plate of our soul guidance. Do we hear it calling us to true happiness? And our soul guidance resists the need to control outcomes. It is a meshing and surrender of your will to divine will. To look at the bigger picture unfolding and let go.

Travel within the vastness of your own being that wants all that is good and worthy of your divinity to open to you. Transcend the belief that all is not possible. One by one, eradicate the limited beliefs you carry within yourself that have held you back all this time from achieving your full potential as a soul being of pure divine light. That is all that deciphers us as human beings, how much of this light we can hold and express out. For light is pure energy in its very nature able to cut through all the confusion and illusions of hatred. So rise up to the occasion of soul mastery and watch the universe conspire to help you in every way possible and perceivably impossible.

- **9.10.21**

Sending out healing energy into the ether.

The power to connect with this energy depends on you and your openness to receive it. The world is going through a crash course in energy clearing. All that has blocked us up to this point is going to be eradicated. All that has stood in the path of your soul will diminish in strength. The weight of the baggage has and still is being lifted. Walk among the earth free now dear one. There is no dream you cannot reach. All is attainable. The mind plays tricks and creates illusions. Focus on what is good, not what is bad. For even the bad is playing with a purpose. For the darkness cannot exist without the light getting even stronger. There will come a time when the darkness will cease to exist in its power. Until then, the struggle is real. And the real fight jihad is against yourself. From the false illusions you have created by yourself.

This world is only but a reflection of what you have created. Step up and claim your dominion over your own territory. For this fight far exceeds what you can do in the physical. It expands out into the universal principles of all things. Made equal and balanced in all ways. When you are whole. All else will fall into place. You are a match for all that you are. And choose to be in this moment. Step up and take your power back. For it belongs to you and only you. Live it, do it, breath it, and most of all really believe it.

Contradictions will keep us stuck until we wholeheartedly step forward with full faith and motion. Believe that all is possible for you love. For the world exists just for you in your devotion. Devote yourself to the one that so calls you to the presence that lies within you. Pure motion is the only energy that can drive this shift into truly becoming. Align with it, be it, and it shall manifest into being. For the universe holds nothing back from you. But the keys to your own paradise lie with you and only you.

Please be careful what you manifest with your thoughts, emotions, and delusions. This is not a game of cat and mouse. It is a real treasure you are seeking. So act like the real treasure that you are.

- 9.1.21

Gain access to higher perspectives, dear friends, transcend the lower octaves of your limited understanding. Transcend the emotions that bind you. Transcend into the possibility that all things are possible. Transcend into the multiplicity that all is rigged in your favor. Because it truly is, so truly believe it from within. See through the heart that knows you can handle this and take things to a deeper level. Take humanity with you to a deeper level so that they may be free from the shackles of their own minds. All things that limit us are part of ego. All things good and bad are meant to teach us that it's time to come out of our own box. See the world for what it really is: a unified factor of infinite grace that binds us all as one.

Believe in the essence of all of humanity connected at its core to one heart center. And this center breathes life to the very force of all that exists. The more we tap into our own center that is contained within the heart, your higher intelligence will expand. And so you will see from above the mountain how everything is falling into place exactly as it needs to. One step at a time and the world will be changed forever. We need these upheavals and revolutions to occur for the safety of all humans to feel at home. This is a call towards real freedom that connects us back to that center. Come back to your soul, they say, and you will find grace in all that you do. And all that you do will take you there.

Trust that you are being guided for your highest good, and for the highest good of all people as one. No one will be left behind but will be granted their rightful stations. Divided are only those who fall to the folly of their own minds. Believe in the greatness of God, most of all, that there is a far greater intelligence than your own. Tap into that and it shall set you free.

- 8.26.21

The more we expand our horizons to see the light at the end of the tunnel, we can ground it into the physical like water mixed with pure light consciousness. Expect your mind to reveal areas where you still lack confidence in the divine plan unfolding. Expect the pain to reveal unconscious made conscious pent-up baggage. For you must become pure like water to see the true mirror of who you really are and what is really unfolding for you. No one should convince you otherwise, including your own shadow self. Lessons around restrictions are being highlighted. Transcend them by tapping into your own uniqueness in blending in with all that is unfolding. And all that is unfolding is indeed part of the divine plan. Step into your knowing now and veil yourself from all that stifles your path. The mirror is on *You* to make that happen.

- **8.23.21**

"The realization of the shadow' is what real spirituality is all about. The more we integrate it, the more we have the ability to be in the vibration of real dolphins, who pick up on real knowledge- that is not only beneficial to our own unique soul growth but we start to not use it in abusive ways to serve that same shadow that we so need to acknowledge and work through for our own highest good and the good of others. Otherwise, it can become a destructive force that will manipulate us in all ways to get that ultimate praise that the ego so loves to feed on, and that is power.

- **6.19.21**

Live up to your highest truth, dear one. Help will come directly from the Source. If only you believed in the power of your own uniqueness. Step up to the plate and make a difference, in the way you were meant to make. Step up to your soul's calling, and watch miracles unfold. Within the silence, there is a deception waning in on your soul. The angels ask that you let go of this burden and lighten into the ever-expansive qualities of your infinite soul capacity. There is no reward greater than witnessing this. You are truly loved, and you know this.

Move forward now with grace, and let no fear or doubt touch you. Blessed be your path, for thou art supported in infinite ways beyond what humans have ever known. The wind will carry you- you will see. The sun and moon serve as your mirror. Awaken to this knowing of infinite grace working in your favor. For thou art have become soul, and soul is above all.

- **4.5.21**

Divine cosmic being of wonder and magic, do you know who you truly are?

Step up to the plate and be aligned with your higher self that is connected to the miraculous unfolding of the universe itself. A small price to pay to let die what no longer serves our higher purpose/ calling. Embrace the infinite wisdom that all is possible, and all it takes is a little bit of reflecting and doing with good intentions. The more real it is, the higher the frequency, the more penetrable the impact/force. To get you to believe and become aligned with the recognition of this infinite self requires dedication to the spiritual mission- which is YOU- all packed inside which contains the whole universe and God in infinite form manifesting in you and everyone around you, reflecting the true meaning of Oneness.

- 10.27.20

Each obstacle facilitates us to look beyond the veil at the ever-flowing wisdom of it all. To look- that the obstacle itself is a gift beyond comparison. To find ourselves is not an easy task at hand, yet the process is just as rewarding. We plan, but the Divine has a greater plan. All the little steps we take, and the pitfalls we may face help us to see a better picture of where we still need work. To heal those wounds by lifting our spirit with what it really needs: a sense of presence with oneself. A union that makes you whole, that sends a signal all across the universe to bring you the comfort and support you truly need. And that comes with true power: The warrior within that breaks through all obstacles. The humble within knows its limits. All in a perfect balance of servant and Master, created and Creator. We are meant to live on earth to know that we are weak as much as we are divine. Hu-man in all forms.

- **8.20.20**

The art of healing has to occur within us before it can occur outside of us. The further away we separate ourselves from others, as so called different in the illusionary sense, the more duality we will create all around us. Visualizing that we are part of a whole, allows us to see that everything is connected in a divine cosmic balance. The only way we will liberate ourselves from our own separation dilemmas, is by knowing that we only see but a fraction of what really is happening. Ultimately, we cannot grasp the whole picture. Submitting to the greater unfolding not only brings inner peace but brings inner wisdom into seeing that real liberation can only occur at an individual level of knowing oneself, thus knowing all of creation, and ultimately 'The One Creator' of it all that has made everything in perfection.

- **8.16.20**

Compassion is not something we magically achieve. It takes a whole uprooting of our own inner pride and molded into refined pieces of a jigsaw puzzle. All past, present, and future incidences play a part in realizing our own weaknesses. That is when we realize we are all really the same. May it be with our addictions that manifests in different forms or power play of good and evil, egos ultimately are all the same. God does not choose who to love or not to love. Like the sun that gives warmth to all. Of course there are ranks among men and women of higher and lower caliber. Yet given the experience in my shoes or your shoes, we would all be struggling in very similar ways. Our strength in entering through that door ultimately is about how merciful and kind we are to ourselves and others. Regardless of what others do or not do for you. Embodiment is crucial in this interplay. Make it unconditional.

- **8.5.20**

The shadow will be no more. The shadow will be turned into light. As your purity overrides everything. Come, come, wherever you are. Oh, wanderer mystic, jewel of creation. The shadow submits to the light within. Your ascension with oneness with the holy inner light will guide you. Follow, and you shall receive all the help you need. A miraculous unfolding prevails you now. Come, come, my beautiful warrior heart. You have so much more heavenly gifts to receive and to experience. There is no turning back now, there is only up…

- **7.10.20**

The expansion into 5D is growing stronger, as the 3D begins to loosen its grip. Calling all light beams to hold your soul calling strong during this time of immaculate change. The angels of your mirror reality applaud you for all the work you've done thus far. As above, so below shall come to pass. Those who have aligned with their star reality must shine their light fully now with no hesitations. The Force is with you dear one, you are never alone.

- **6.21.20**

You are your own greatest love first. Believe in the power of your own belief about yourself. Get out of your own way, as some like to say. When you doubt yourself and your abilities are questioned, sometimes in your own mind, stop to ponder what the belief blocks are within yourself that are creating that restriction in my reality. Conquer that mindset or lack of and illuminate through your own blocks. Shine a light on your own demons. Cleanse your aura of any negativity. The light bulb isn't going to dim unless you turn off the light switch yourself. Keep your belief in yourself alive no matter what. And believe in that greater divinity working through you. If we constantly align with our own light, surely God will illuminate and support us in every way possible.

- **1.30.20**

We're given exercises to increase our patience and resilience to follow the light in the face of darkness. Some of us are trained all our lives for this. The greater the soul task, the greater the tests become. Yet we are never given more than we can handle. They know we're strong enough to carry. Treasures come to those who are patient, which then transforms into new levels of peaceful patience. Through all the invisible support, we know we can do this. We know what tremendous treasures it will open. It's as worth it as the Sun being compared to the tiny stars in the darkness. There is absolutely no comparison. We delve into the knowing of this, which brings so much peaceful contentment.

- **1.16.20**

The underlying presence of a Creator uplifts us to fly like a butterfly. With each snowflake uniquely imprinted with angelic water codes that descend as living light codes of illumination and transcendence. And those who embody the frequency/awareness that God is always with them become special human beings that eventually learn how to fly becoming more and more beautiful in that awareness as they heal and become uplifted that God is always taking care of them, while absorbing the frequencies of these codes that descend like frozen vibrations in time. Yet the very lack of awareness that God is not present with us makes us fall. As we ourselves embody this angelic secret of always being aware of our Creator, it allows for an invisible support system of angelic beings to help us along the way in our ascension towards the heavens. Reaching new heights of joy, love, and trust, and as we delve deeper in the knowing that we are always carried.

- **12.17.19**

There is always something pushing us to go further into addicting realities like a moth to a flame, a driving force of love almost as if you've become possessed. Treasures given on one condition that you will get burned and that you stay on the path of slowly burning away your selfish ego. Annihilation is easy to talk about so let's not talk about it, someone once said. It's surely not a butterfly yet, because it's still got a lot of healing to do. Rewards of endless treasure openings, the closer you get, the more you want to get burned because the rewards/ tastes are heavenly in nature. A process that makes us completely transparent and light like a moth. The only thing it knows is that it's being taken to the source of light. The sun shams appears so near, yet so far.

- **9.16.19**

Rise above duality, rise above conditioning. We were born to carry this rainbow light within our vessels and transmute the conundrums of ego and surrounding dark energy refocused into light. We were born to rise above shallow notions of what's right and wrong and go deeper in our understanding of who we are and what we came here for. We were born leaders to be of service to true spirituality. Bringing rainbow consciousness as heaven on earth, through our unconditional love for our Beloved and unity with their perfect light. We need two wings to fly above these illusions. We need one eye to see unity.

- **7.28.19**

When everything in your life comes to teach you: trust in Allah (God). The essence of all of existence, to let go of our own control and embrace the most merciful change that is taking place in every moment, to get us to rise up and up always up. Always carried, never by our own effort, yet this gift waits for us to be open to receive it and really truly believe it. That there is a power far beyond our own understanding that carries through like an invisible heavenly wind far beyond what this material world could ever do.

- **4.26.19**

Like a library with many levels of knowledge, clouds of existence/absorption, I think the reason behind why our prayers don't get answered is because we dwell in low vibes. Even sometimes we may not even be aware of it because so many unconscious issues within us are playing out that don't make intention cut clear. It does not align us with attracting the best outcome that resides in the higher planes. Unless we can reach those higher planes of existence within and without, our lives will keep replaying the same old drama scenes on repeat. Miracles happen in the higher planes. Like many layers of music, the first level plays the most untuned inharmonious one and as we ascend the music becomes more fine-tuned and harmonious. Whatever we align with, with our own energy and way of being, is what we will attract. Positive thinking and always thinking of the best outcome in everything we do, is not a simplistic way of looking at the world, it is a divine way of looking at it.

The question is, which dimension do we dwell in?

- **4.2.19**

The void and conflict that our minds create, is the same conflict that others' mirrors reflect. Thoughts are very powerful, to the point that they create vacuums of disillusionment and disempowerment, bringing upon us the very things that are in conflict in our minds. Outer reality reflects this so much. Oftentimes, keeping us in a loop/ void. There are so many new colors/ vibrations of the rainbow we can align with, if only we choose to. Constantly aware that our reality can shift any time because our mind and mood will create it and contain it. Time is really an illusion. Align with the rainbow reality, where all things beautiful are possible. In such a crummy world, we need it. One by one we can change the world!

- 1.16.19

Your optimistic energy personality is shifting the very fabric of reality. Be a diamond in the rubble. Shift your focus to all that is beautiful and work on making all that is not beautiful. Not tomorrow but today. Today! Be your own muse, your own savior, your own warrior. Treasures lie when we dig deep. The deeper the swim, the more magnificent the treasures. Candy is for kids. Mystical Jewels are for those who seek. Sticky icky ego please let us BE, so that we may shine our light even brighter!

- **1.9.19**

Do we realize that we are made of stars, a diamond reality that seeks to shine through our skin? Do we seek to follow the light wherever we go? Do we seek to know what that reality is? Waiting to unlock from within, magnificent diamond light codes of extreme beauty. Our innate sense of loving light gives us a glimpse of that reality. We must seek it. Incomparable to all the lights contained in this world. Soul light transcends all lights.

- **12.23.18**

To achieve great things, ego has to be left behind. Open to the power of the soul! How tricked we are into thinking that this world and our selfish needs mean anything. Until we've gone down a rabbit hole in attempts to save ourselves from the enemy, only to realize we didn't bring a ladder to get out. The soul will give you wings to fly. If only we knew that suffering unlocks this power. And you will need nothing else. Be and it shall be anything you wish! Great things glow. Spiral yourself to infinity. Soul sparks multiplied.

- **29/11/18**

Rather than worry about what is lost, build on what is new. Every day is a new day. We always try and fail. Sincerity is what drives us and is our only savior. Only God is perfect. Only God is Great. To think otherwise is fallacy. Everything we go through in life is to teach us patience and humility. To break us down until only the soul is left. That's where we belong, and that's where we shall stay, no matter what we achieve. Purity is what we seek. The Sun is always shining, no matter what happens. Thank goodness for His infinite Mercy.

- **10.31.18**

As long as black finds itself superior to white, or white finds itself superior to black, it will never see the other in its pureness fullness. Between expansion and contraction, the void is where the light enters. Both reside in the center as equals, in perfect proportion, with no illusions of separation. Illuminated in each other's presence. One cannot exist without the other. The interchanging between black and white, plus and minus charge is what makes the whole world whole. It is what creates movement, creates gold.

- 10.24.18

Painting and visualizing a golden shield against all negativity and resistance for all that stand for love. Real peace comes from within. When good and evil is made manifest. Truth is never easy to witness. Between expansion and contraction, balance and proportion, the world's in perfect order.

- **10.22.18**

Yes you are worthy to eat good food, you are worthy to sit and read a book, you are worthy to be loved, you are worthy to have all that you dream of. Never underestimate yourself or anyone. We are all worthy of the highest form of love and compassion. First to ourselves, then only then, can we truly learn to treat others that way.

- **10.16.18**

You are a wild child my love. Never to be shackled by the chains of this life. Feel free to open to the mysteries of who you are. This is not a practical joke. Come out of your mind and come out to play because there's a mind field of diamonds waiting for you to penetrate. Mirroring you. If only you knew what we have in store for you. You would jump right in.

- 10.5.18

You are amazing and always will be. Don't let the past spoil the honey milk that you are. Let's live truly in the now so we can clearly see. There was nothing ever wrong except for in our minds. Cleansing and clearing away the debris so now we can see. Imagine me to be whatever you want me to be and that I am. Your wish is always granted. Ask from within. From a place that's truly healed. If you embody it, I will be it too.

- **10.3.18**

Stand in your power, oh majestic one! You are beautiful, you are light. You have so much potential to be incredible! Step up into the center of your eternal existence. Love love love like crazy! This ocean is too deep to ever look back. Let it wash you, let it purify you, let it caress you. Let it take all your sense of self and burdens away. Let it open you to the power of one.

- **4.16.18**

Touch it, see there is no wall between you and the other side that is love. Tap into it any time you feel like it. Let it allow your heart to open and infinitely expand. You are a divine being of light. When you embody love, you become all that is, and are able to penetrate your surroundings like the wind. Embody love, for it has an invisible effect, and opens portals you never imagined even existed. You are truly limitless if you just believe in yourself. The world is only but an outer covering, a dense forest designed to see if you will follow your own light. Enter through the gate of eternity. Do what is eternal.

- **3.7.18**

The real question is- what am I doing to attract certain situations into my life? Energy speaks louder than words, always- and situations that arise always come to shed a light on what it is we ourselves need to work on. Our mind is more powerful than we think. Feed it calmness and so it shall give you calmness. As within so without.

- **1.24.18**

"Listen to your heart, it knows all things, because it came from the soul of the world and it will one day return there."

The more you listen the more it will expand and one day it will open to you a treasure it's been so patiently waiting to give you. Sad that we don't seek; slow but worth the wait if we do. Oh, what a joy it will be when you discover it. A world within manifesting a world without- all things engulfed by the essence of our soul. Enter where you shall receive from its infinite flowers of grace.

- **12.10.17**

Depending on our level of understanding and noticing subtleties, the more we will notice perceived flaws. As our perception cleanses, the more those very flaws become mercies. Because if there wasn't anything to correct, what are we living for anyway? This process and journey of refinement is the whole essence of life itself. If there is no struggle or hard work applied to improve what the reward for anyway? It doesn't exist then does it? Paradise does not come free but needs a reason to enter. Dark/ light, hot/ cold, plus/minus exist simultaneously; otherwise, they would cancel each other out. And the better we do in the midst of evil the more reward we get. That's just how the cosmic scales tip and much like an algebra formula.

- **11.28.17**

Reality is never as it appears. The inner versus outer colors of which are always different. Sometimes what our body finds enjoyable is not always the case of what our soul wants from us. A contradiction in the same pot that comes up to a boil. Emotions such as sadness reflect that. As long as we do our part in goodness, God takes care of the rest. Trust that He will bring out the best outcome in any situation. It is your own inner sincerity and piety that reigns in the end. If your tire gets flat it means you were not meant to go down that road anyway. Take it as a mercy and try another. And soon you shall find your soul's purpose and true inner happiness.

"Don't be sad, God is with us."

- **11.2.17**

Trust in the invisible and the unexpectedness far beyond what we could ever figure out or fix ourselves. There is a higher power at work here, which our minds will never understand. Leaving it to us and our own efforts would be like walking around wearing an old grey sweatshirt that's inside out looking all silly, because that's all we found. Trust that they will give from a love so pure, like a father hugging his daughter. Just when we're done looking for it, we receive the most perfect gift, and certainly not what we expected. All things beautiful glow and you will know.

- **8.11.17**

A Human being is like a leaf. For every leaf has to change color and fall in order to bring forth the new. Ever changing with the seasons from fall to winter to spring to summer. What matters is our remembrance of the Divine. Imprint of His Oneness on all things living, the eternal, the absolute. The One who created it all and can change it all too. La illaha illah Huu.

- **11.8.16**

The process of awakening to our true soul's purpose is an ever-unfolding journey, like a lotus flower unfolding then closing and opening once again. Each cycle of rebirth reveals something different. It requires much beating up of the physical shell to make it possible though: trials and tribulations, harsh conditions, much inner work, introspection and unlearning what we have learned at times to make room for the new. If the seed keeps dancing above the ground being swayed by the wind of illusions to and fro, how will it ever become that lotus? Unless it's planted in the dirt of seclusions and nurtured proper soul fuel it surely won't grow. For darkness precedes the dawn. The seed is always dying inside to be reborn, will we not let it shine in the sunlight? In love and divine care it will, if only we let it, trust and surrender like all things in nature do. The day it first sprouts from the ground is a site to be seen. Unimaginable of its splendor, the feeling of a new world emerging from the unseen. Surely that time in the underworld is much worth it in the end, and it will be dancing in its full glory. Not just as a seed though, but as a beautiful ever blooming inspiring lotus, till eternity.

- **9.20.16**

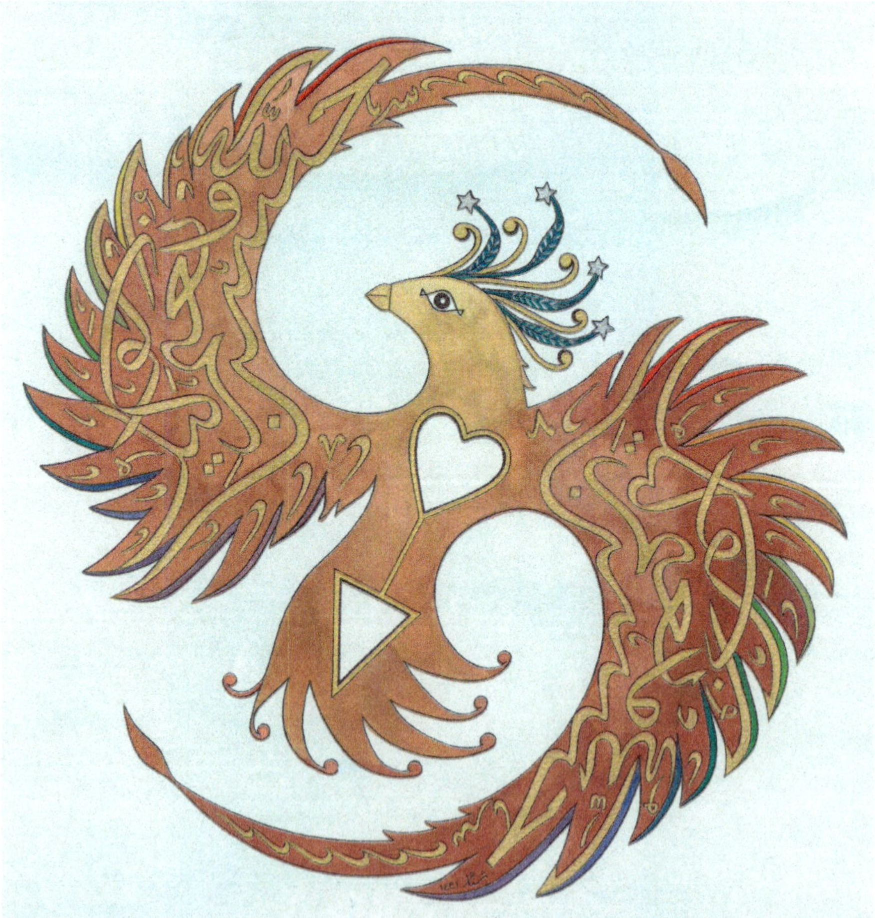

II

The Entering

"Seek the treasure and you shall find a glory beyond measure."

Align with the Divine and your own embodiment of the divine. You truly can create and bend reality to serve you in every given moment. Trust the divine timing of how things are unfolding because it is building you up to the highest version of you and the most immaculate ascension journey towards the greatest mountain of light.

- 2.10.23

If we just look with true vision we will see the wisdom of the wholeness of a masterpiece unfolding oh so perfectly in conjunction to our souls' promised mastery. The straight path is oh so straight and narrow yet infinite in its potential. Unity with divine self is the ultimate goal. If you are present, the path will seem shorter as time is non-existent when you're in a light-ness of be-ing. Your path is high, and the soul knows no confusion but moves with a gracious certainty. Look into that with a beautiful grin that you're treading the path of ultimate freedom within self and the mirror that is all a reflection of you. Embrace the union of polarities in all things and allow for the openings to show you the oneness in everything. Merge the ego with golden soul self, as you expand and embody new beginnings in each moment. Present and whole in all ways.

- **4.21.23**

The ultimate path of truth is all about awakening to your innocence, Fitra and that has a lot to do with ultimate embodiment of true humility, peace, and compassion. Because ultimately all of humanity is opening up to their true human self, and the path can look different for each one of us on how we get there. It is a destination of levels (energy frequency into more and more light) as we clear our own heaviness or choose to hold onto it. Knowing that you truly do have a mystical horse spirit being buraq carries you if you so allow it. Look to the wisdom of the unfolding of it all as the ultimate vision of expansion being made manifest here on earth.

Sure, it takes time to ground heavenly energy, as we peel away the layers of conditioning but surely it is happening. Raise your vibe in terms of true clarity, peace, and non-judgement. That will be the very gauge of how well you will be able to receive these higher heavenly codes to infuse your body and consciousness. Be open minded, not literal in your approach. Be in submission not attack mode and all will work out in your ultimate favor. Be the dancing Phoenix of Balance- strong and resilient yet relaxed and far stretching into the infinite expansiveness of the universal void.

Embrace it all in true oneness.

- **3.24.23**

The dissolving light is unlearning all that you knew and becoming completely new in every moment. We are ascending towards a path of greater awareness of ourselves and thus knowing and aligning with our divine selves. Whatever contradictions arise, you trust your own journey to greater wholeness. If you don't integrate it now, it will come to haunt you sooner or later. It is important to embrace our dark and light and come out the healthiest version of ourselves. All aspects of ourselves that have been repressed need to be integrated for proper evolution into higher timelines.

- **3.3.23**

Tap into that universal consciousness that knows that all things are connected. There is a divine wisdom in all that unfolds, good and bad. The lesson of oneness is the real journey and spirituality and all religions combined. Release the separateness and embrace the oneness.

- **2.3.23**

You've travelled long and far to come to this point of great healing. Resist the urge to manifest lower versions of yourself that you once knew but no longer exist anymore. Embrace the cosmic shift that is aligning you with higher versions of yourself. Be prepared to let go of any stuck energy that doesn't allow you to move forward. Release the density of others' pain around you and be a channel for higher vibration always. Your mission is disrupted when you give into the illusions of the toxic nature of your surroundings.

What if I were to tell you that you could control how much you absorb of this negativity? You are more magnificent than you think you are. Your light outshines way beyond what the shadow tries to bind unto. It is like the sun that tries to fit into the space of a small room. Sooner or later the light shines through the windows and illuminates all to see. You cannot contain the sun. For the sun illuminates you. For those who try to put a shadow on the sun will only fall into more and more darkness. Be weary the of nature of this light. It is infinite and magnifies ten-fold to the strength of your own intention and which direction you take it. Let go of all subconscious fears as they come up from the intensity of what this light illuminates. Breathe in the deep calling that speaks through your soul.

And don't worry about the 3-dimensional worldly success. It is only an illusion that distracts from the more infinite goal. That which is for your highest evolution is be-ing grounded here on earth. The transmutation is finally complete. When you have become calm as water in the most still vessel. Be gold and you will remain impenetrable. Where gold exists, impurities resist and cannot co-exist. You shall forever be turned into gold. For this is the ultimate mission of your existence. Be true to thee.

- **10.30.22**

The Treasure Within

You are a mirror of all that you are. Oh, you who believe, believe more- that is the sail that drives the force. The more you visualize the highest outcome, the more it shows up for you in real time. The divine in me sees the divine in you. And our inner peace and knowing above all else reflects and will be the means of our higher freedom being unlocked in greater levels. We are fueled by Source itself. And that magical unicorn buraq does exist and will carry you there. It will appear in the form of spiritual uplifting energy, so pay attention to those subtle signs that are so often not sensed because of the stronger, more overpowering outside illusive forces that distract us. Nothing is as it seems at this point. Follow the dream not the illusion, as it merges more and more into your physical reality. Art is alive, and so is the spirit behind it, and so are you a spiritual being that penetrates through all space, time and dimension.

Signs signs, pay attention to the signs- they serve as oracles of higher truths in sync with your higher mind.

- **9.21.22**

You don't need a change in scenery to make things happen. You need a change in inner wisdom. As within so without will follow divine will if you so be it yourself. Know thyself to know your mirror. No projections just injections of a cosmic knowledge that all is rigged in your favor. No worries if others don't see, you experience it. And so the story unfolds into infinity. Where you rise, all rise in the most interconnected way. Don't underestimate the process of your own well-being becoming more and more perfect. Focus on your own healing and what brings you internal joy. And all will be revealed in due time in parallel.

As you open, doors open. Your own light will illuminate the path. You will see how all doors lead to one. It requires you to be beyond this world but still of it. Time is ascending as you are ascending. You know the lessons you have learned thus far unfolding into the bigger picture. Do you see through the eyes of God? The path is never linear but always multidimensional. Keep going, for you will reach eternal freedom. Beyond attachments, form, and illusions of a lower nature. Eternal happiness is attained from within and manifests without. Remember that dear one. And you shall remain centered in Hu-man infinite possibilities.

- **9.12.22**

Look for the cosmic gift in everything. Look for the radiance that is your soul. Look for the blooming of the infinite flower within you and all things. All is but a lesson, learn to listen to the eternal truths manifesting themselves through you in all ways. In whatever way you need, the guide will appear to show you the way to your highest calling. Stay present now and know that the higher path is unravelling for you always. If you see it or not, it is always working in your favor. See the mercy and wisdom of everything. Seek and you shall find whatever you focus on. Make it infinite then ground it in physical form- Hu-man form with an eternal sky of infinite possibilities, formless yet forkful at the same time. All is a parody of the whole destiny unfolding.

- **9.9.22**

Embrace the magic that your higher self brings to you. Don't be fooled by the lower perceived notions of yourself. You are infinitely beautiful in every way. The fountain of youth is when time stops and you keep loving. Stay in love where your blissful energy resides. If you fall, it will raise a hand, heart, and energy to gently bring you back up. This love loves you unconditionally. It has no gains of fame or recognition of any kind. It just loves to love you in every dream-able way possible- for you. It knows no distance between us. It only celebrates the union that is our right in this moment and every moment.

You deserve the best and you know it. You deserve to be recognized by the highest version of you. That knows no boundaries to this infinite most expansive love. You know what this love means to you. Bathe in all its bliss. Because heaven is right here on earth. Where you have a dream-heart becomes the very vessel. For the prophecy is true. You have become Love. By its infinite nature. Be and it shall be whatever you like and have dreamed of and much, more than you have ever imagined. The love that is yours to take if you so wish.

- **9.4.22**

*D*on't underestimate the power of divine intervention in your life- I repeat again.

Shift your mindset to be open to receiving this saving. Do you see how you've been trapped by your own limited views? And created a world exactly based on those very views. A world that mirrors you and you don't even realize you were the cause of it. Release the view, and the circumstance changes. All it takes is awareness back to self and it will work like magic. Try it on small things then gradually learn to shift big things. If you have a block towards higher guides intervening and advising in your life, look to the root of the cause of your mistrust. For it comes from a place where you think you run the show. Nothing is by accident, remember that, for it is all playing out for your highest good. Trust and be entrusted. For your good or bad reality is a mirror of how much you trust.

Don't make hasty decisions based on temporary phases of ambitions or desires in your life. But look to what you have always been deep down as a roadmap to avoid what is not you. Don't be conditioned by the outside. Threats can be misleading. And emotional reactions can only serve as signposts to your healing. Watch for the blind spots, for the higher guidance will reveal those in due time as you need them. Listen to the silent cautious voice that is not of the mind but that of the heart. For it will forewarn you. For that is your guide speaking through you. You know exactly what it means in your particular life or situation that calls you. Do you care to listen?

Your work is done to integrate dark forces, now it's back to the light.

- **7.15.22**

Open that portal for you to jump into the next stage of your evolution. Don't underestimate the power of divine intervention in your life. For it will come to sweep you off your feet when you least expect it. Like a dark night dressed in red, it seems to be out of place. In the morning in pure daylight, as the light settles in. As the mystery unfolds, you too shall be one with all that you thought was for your folly. Shakespeare speaks to you through the eloquence of his tongue. Your higher self knows only harmony- remember that. Harmonic motions unite you. Stir the pot enough times in steady circular motions. Go into the portal and bring back the timeline that once was your highest destiny. It can be once again, if you so let it enter through the cracks of your misguided soul. Enter the stellar gateway of your heart, where the wisdom of true happiness has always been. Nothing compares to The Sun.

- **7.12.22**

Do you smell the flowers around you that reflect the garden that you are? Do not underestimate the power of your heart, my love. For it has the ability to channel great distances into timelines that never before existed. Your abilities far exceed the normal threshold of what is considered human. For it is angelic in nature, that pierces through the dimension of density so fast like light laser beams. Your task is not to seek it outside of you now, but to seal the union that you most desire in the heavens of your mind unto planet earth. It is not something you can gain through logic or planning but entails a greater calling of a higher wisdom of manifestation through pure love for self and other as one. That energy will be your guide for what is false and what is illusion.

Carry on as you did so peacefully before and know that no harm will ever reach you. Unless you let it in, through those cracks of your past that have kept you so chained in regret and worry. Release that now and know that all is well because it truly is- oh master of your own reality. Come witness thy power now. For you want to gain your true destiny. Seek and you shall find- for it has all been within you, this whole time and beyond time.

Be and it shall be, if you so desire it.

- **7.10.22**

Imagine yourself being inside a bubble of cosmic mercy, constantly shaping itself to give you exactly what you need in every way. Amidst the chaos, there is cosmic wisdom that nourishes the whole, happening on a grander scale. Don't see situations as restrictions but opening in some way. Flip the mind's eye from the duality of I versus you but that of pure mercy. God's mercy is infinite, we just don't see it sometimes. Imagine infinite creation and connection of your own being as one with your surroundings. Then congratulate yourself, for you have just learned how to mold matter into your own hands. Mold it, program it- to be one with you.

- **6.21.22**

Being in true love is the only energy that can open our perception to see beyond the masks of ego illusion that makes us think that our reality is in some sort of imperfection. And misunderstandings about and lack of real submission and peace only arises because we cannot see beyond what the ego wants. Slowly tame/ silence the ego, and the eternal reality of situations starts to unveil themselves. There are far greater arrangements being made than we can perceive with our limited 3D vision. Ego does not see the eternal bigger picture/ nature of things, nor the deep healing, energy clearing and stamina that has to be built to reach what is required of you for the future. If you lose your breath halfway climbing up the mountain, who's going to save you if you get stuck and haven't fully prepared for what awaits you on the top and the other side?

God knows what you need to heal now, and the time that seem like delays are blessings for whatever you truly wish for. In essence, everything happening even now is what you wished for. Because ascension is reached in steady grounded steps and the wings and the higher vision we are granted are meant to keep us truly patient and grateful for all that is happening now. To know that the wait is not time wasted but precious preparation. And learning the art of being is what it's all about anyway. We know that everything is perfectly aligned for what we need now. And when things are meant to be, they will be. What is meant to be, will be. God's Will be done. Trust. Infinitively trust and the perception to see why things are as they are will open more and more.

- **5.26.22**

The raw nature of your be-ing speaks to you in pure form. Listen to the call of your soul. Respect yourself to the fulfilment of your mission in every way that opens. Be ready to ground wherever you can. Don't underestimate the power of purpose driven by love. For the effects of it may not be fully visible to the naked eye. But the reality of its energy transcends way beyond what you can fathom. If you believe that you are one with your soul, then rejoice in the knowing that you have become part of a greater divine plan unfolding. The witnessing of you as the miracle will transmute the doubt that is made to seem real.

You are a divine being of cosmic light emanating throughout the vast crevices of the universe. Bring back the last remnants of the fragmented parts of your soul together again. Witness the miracle that is you once again, as a mirror of heaven on earth. You better believe it. Or all else will fail to show you in comparison. Don't judge yourself. Be kind. For how far you have come to reach your highest destination. Flowers will bind you forever more as your sustenance. Trust that you will be carried. As much as you will ground, all else will be taken care of. Trust most of all in yourself to be entrusted. And the dissolving of unnecessary timelines will happen over time. And in a moment unexpected and expected, the tables will turn to be all in your favor.

- **4.4.22**

The heart contains the treasure, the closeness of the wonder and majesty of it all. The ascension journey that knows no bounds, transcends beyond physical distance. Your heart surely knows how to guide you to your ultimate destiny. Seek the treasure and you shall find a glory beyond measure. The ascent into the vastness of your own soul, where you remain untouchable to the collective noise. Where you hear the angels calling you to divine oneness in a physical body that transcends all obstacles. You can do it, they say, keep moving towards your heart. You know the way to the higher dimensions of the magic that still awaits you. Keep seeking and you shall find the treasures that still remain dormant, yet to be explored.

- **2.9.22**

The piece where this whole journey all began, and where it is joining- who knew, in the greatest divine story ever to be told. The very vehicle that connected us, will be the same one that will connect us yet again. All in divine timing, it is really happening. The green island is approaching and there's nothing anyone can do but for us to prepare for the greatest arrival of hearts. A culmination of an energy so powerful to lift the sea up to the heavens and grounded on this very planet. We worked and trained all our lives for this. Every moment of pain brought a new opening and all the love brought us closer to understanding what real belief, oneness, and true love really means. I wouldn't trade it for the world. This spiritual connection in deeper oceans, mystical and physical realities yet to unfold.

- **11.17.21**

The secret of the secret is hidden within the unexpected where no one would possibly look. So obvious yet so hidden because we are so deeply conditioned to judge based on 3D criteria. Only a heavenly mind and a pure and open heart can see how everything is connected to the secret of oneness that permeates through all. This is not rocket science, it's spiritual science that requires a soul rocket to understand and really experience. And neither is it a secret you can read in books and just get because you may be an intellectual or smarter than the rest. The secret of the secret lies in the heart of a true believer who really believes and has really tasted what it means to truly surrender. To truly live by the flow governed by the ship of safety that keeps you from faltering into your own self-help perpetuating blind spots. Real spirituality requires a guide, a real chain linking all the way back to the source which is the fountain that keeps flowing in the now forever more. The ink will never dry out, tasting the reality of true humility that you are absolutely nothing in this ocean, yet everything at the same time.

- **11.5.21**

The more open you are to allowing things to unfold naturally, as they always want to in your favor, you will see that you were coming in your own way all along. There is no magic potion for attaining this elixir of magic in your life, but to simply allow what comes your way to unfold in the way that it needs to without pushing your own limits on things and situations. Be present in the moment to be ready to truly trust that all is always rigged in your favor- and that's a fact. God is real and all that is good is always waiting to reach you, if you so remain open to receive it.

- **9.28.21**

When the divine wants you to carry out a mission, don't expect it to be easy at times. Submission, sacrifice, and sincerity for the greater good will continue to call you to stay aligned with it. That becomes your straight and narrow path. As much as it may be hard to follow fully in the beginning, it becomes easier later on as your body and mind align with the great call of the soul. It takes time for the unravelling to happen of that greater purpose. Although some of us have always consciously been aware of this 'service to humanity' all our lives yet discover more and more that we play a major part in this. Serving as a conduit for a greater purpose and really aligning with that most of all brings forth a union of souls so immense, the treasure of it cannot be fathomed. Continuing towards it forever more- never taking on pennies for gold. For gold is our path that will lead us in those infinite directions of so many beautiful openings to come.

- **3.6.21**

Trust in God that the road will be made easy to ascend into higher versions of our Sunlight. Every day is a new day. Conquer all limitations with honesty, humbleness, and conviction, and the soul will be allowed to shine brighter and brighter, as the ego becomes weaker and weaker. "Tune in to the portal of your heart." The heart is expanding like the sky. The merging of body and heart is allowing for a vaster vista of opportunities to be revealed. Fill it with whatever you dream of and yet again let the heart dream it. There is a far greater divine plan unfolding than we can ever even imagine for ourselves. Trust the unveiling invisible magic unfolding layer by layer. Trust in the process!

- **11.16.20**

Let the Kundalini rise, and the divine energy soar you to new heights within yourself. As your heart awakens to the majestic qualities of who you really are. As your light body encapsulates your physical being. As your physicality becomes more and more run by the soul more and more. Slowly integrating your entire being to new and higher timelines. Uplifting humanity and bringing in new pathways to explore and become born to. And manifest in the New World, more harmonious and integrated.

- **11.10.20**

When the heart flutters from one place to another, the golden path is revealed to the mystics of the unseen realm. There is no comparison to the beauty of angelic wings we are granted when we let go of ego and embrace the infinite unknown perfection that is always all around us. Do we seek to find flaws in that Creator's perfection, or do we embrace what is revealed to be a gift in disguise? You choose your reality, what you want it to be. And that is the real definition of a friend of the infinite One God, One Source within us all. Embrace the divinity in all, so you can see how magical life can really be. Away from illusion, away from all drama.

- **9.7.20**

Is there a purpose to everything? Of course there is. Is there a precise programmed plan that unfolds? Of course there is. Is there a hidden order in all that looks like chaos? Of course there is.

And yet our free will acts within the confines of an immaculate flower of life. A universe within a universe, all in planned glory. Do we not witness the sun and moon perfectly aligned when it is their time. Each day, everyday revolving as one. The cosmic dance of the interplay of light and dark, shadow and no shadow, free flow and organization, free will and planned balanced proportions. It creates the perfect balance of body and soul intermingling, of higher knowing and integration, of balance and proportion, of ease and dis-ease. Reaching new heights in our understanding that all is a beautiful unfolding of perfection.

- **8.18.20**

Your soul will always guide you to what it wants to physically manifest. Take time to explore your inner treasures and the sky within you. As we become one with our light body angelic self, we open the door to experience the vision of divine beauty and majesty all around us. As we unveil ourselves from our masks, we realize that we are not only divine beings of light but here for a purpose to ascend into higher planes of consciousness. While riding on the buraq of our ego, that once tamed, will allow us to fly into new worlds of heavenly freedom.

- **7.30.20**

*E*mbrace the oneness of your own being. See the oneness around you.

One person's strength is another person's weakness. Your strengths will be magnified by the signs and synchronicities you see illuminating what's inside you. And so, will be your weaknesses. What triggers you are reg flags of angelic messages asking you to heal those certain areas. Contemplate the truth that everyone and every situation reflects you. Separation is an illusion. Know that you are exactly where you need to be in this moment of now. So much healing lies in embracing this. Know that you are meant to walk a path that enlightens you with the truth that all is one. Witness the oneness in all things. Nothing unfolds without reason.

Do you really believe in oneness?

- **6.3.20**

The secret of progress sometimes lies in the art of letting go. And where does this divine intervention of letting go take you?

Well, that is something for you to discover. Perhaps the Divine has another plan not so structured around what you planned because after all, that is limited by the mind. If we allowed ourselves to ponder just a little bit at the magnificence that is unfolding in this very moment. Perhaps it is something that we unimaginably thought we could never attain and how could we because our mind couldn't grasp it anyway. The next best thing is to surrender to the flow and all that is, and to see everything rigged in your favor as much as it may look like a curse at first.

Let your mind's inner eye of oneness wander into the wisdom that everything serves a spiritual purpose and is an unravelling and wide spanning of a higher calling. All within a beautiful connectedness. Will you not come with an open mind and an open heart and regain the mysteries of all that is your purpose. To heal yourself and so many around you. To give in to that infinite flow that is always working its magic. A stepping into that ocean of Grace.

The process of ascension may not be easy sometimes as we are faced with new challenges that serve to constantly strengthen those spiritual muscles. Yet what is it about the process of refining these skills that we learn to become humbly aligned with the calling of true love in all its essence. It cannot be attained until our very nature is purified at its core and the very illusions and addictions of ego have been tamed into a remarkable piece of art that is you and all that is star-like. That very interesting polishing that happens to ready you for your ultimate destiny of aligning, transmitting and transferring those very patterns made of pure love to the sky star nature that you are and were always reborn to be. Be ready, be open, because it's all well worth it. In other words, real progress requires real work!

- **5.29.20**

Love is going to catch you in your disguise, open you up like a flower that knows nothing more than to love and be loved admired and appreciated. Once you know the value of what love really is, everything else becomes an illusion of separation from the whole. If it doesn't bring you to remembering of that oneness, then it's not the truth. To align with that truth, you have to unfold all the mysteries within yourself first to be able to see that Love is the only thing that exists. And if we look close enough to that center, we will find that love has always been there all along. So rejoice in the knowing that you are loved and will always be loved. Because the true definition of a flower is the very essence of love itself.

- **5.17.20**

Back to nothingness is where we belong. Anything outside of that doesn't exist. Humankind was made for this one purpose. Locking in that intention is the very core of our dna. It takes time, dedication, witnessing the unfolding of all that is falsehood. A brutal journey at its core, but all so rewarding to see the fruits of your labor manifest in ways you never imagined. Bringing back that color of life to where it really belongs and where it has always been. In the heart of humankind that neither knows existence without pain or sorrow but learns through the ever-evolving wisdom of your soul that knows that every dream is possible to make a reality. Removing those veils one by one to reveal that lush dna that has always made its promise to be revealed to you in this living lifetime as the ultimate reward of the utmost heavenly, grounded in plain site for all to see and rejoice in the knowing that you have finally become one with the one that has always shared this mirror with you.

- **5.13.20**

To gain access to higher levels of understanding/ knowledge of ourselves and others and the way the universe orchestrates itself in the many infinite mysteries, requires constant sacrifice of ego-self. And those who tap into the subtleties of the elemental world realize all is moving in a continuum of perfect order yet appearing as chaos sometimes. We have a choice to either ablaze into the fire or conquer our fears and truly live with testimony that God is the ultimate ruler of affairs. For us to be in acceptance with that fact will allow us to come out alive and even stronger in the end by aligning ourselves with that ultimate truth of divine will. It's so simple yet so difficult at times, since we have an ego that needs dying yet transforming into useful new versions of itself. There is no power or strength except through God, the most high, the most great.

- **1.10.20**

It is very much the energy of knowing we are supported, and moving with the divine flame of life wherever it takes us. Yet the only thing that will keep us moving is this energy of unconditional love we have within us. To become a better person, to achieve greater things, to live up to new and unfound territories that our short-sighted vision has not come to see just yet! It is not so much the choices we will make, for some of us, but the unexpected twists of fate that will be revealed as we rise up into our power of who we are and what we want to become, with a clear direction of where we want to go.

Low level love doesn't cut it for the phoenix. It feels and knows that it deserves so much more! The heart is too ablaze to just sit around on the sidelines. As it awakens to new levels of its own burning heart, it opens doors to new levels of living and loving within self and surrounding. While waking up more and more to its divine nature of no fear. In other words, the rise of the phoenix creates a natural rise in the frequency of what codes it can access and higher dimensions it can open, all in parallel to its own spiritual awakening.

- **1.3.20**

When your heart opens, mirrors appear, showing you your deepest fear, desires, and unlocked potential. Seeing God in everyone. You are the one in whom ego still remains untamed. Blemishing your whole world and how you see it. As the mirror polishes, the site becomes more pure, vast, and perfect. In a beautiful unravelling process. To get you to your target. Of that beautiful palace. Of ultimate essence. One with Rabb and all of creation. Synced together in a triad of "be and it shall be" kun fa ya kun. In perfect harmony.

- **11.3.19**

To create the work that we do and to fully live the purpose we were meant to live in this lifetime, you really have to step back and recalibrate what your priorities are in life, all in balance and alignment with your higher path and calling. When you sit by yourself in those moments of silence, what is it that your heart is calling you to fulfil? In that deep knowing, learn to transcend distractions and go deeper. Know that what you do with your heart and soul is important and really the only thing that's true, despite all the illusions of this world that come to distract you. Own your own light and you will find that the light will work through your body more and more. As the body submits, the head follows, and the heart makes all the magic happen. Our guides are just waiting for us to let go and let God handle what we ourselves are not in control of anyway. Learn to transcend the bounds of illusion and live in your heaven. Your doorway to that ultimate destination of bliss within and without.

- **10.21.19**

Trust in God that the road will be made easy to ascend into higher versions of our Sunlight. Every day is a new day. Conquer all limitations with honesty, humility, and conviction, and the soul will be allowed to shine brighter and brighter, as the ego becomes weaker and weaker.

- **10.7.19**

When the manifestation comes and your heart soars. There's no comparison to this rainbow energy. Let it fly you to new heights and reach you to new potentials. The colors of oneness live strong in the beings of those who devote their lives to purity of divine essence and culmination of spirit. Live and love like a 'Divine Phoenix', because we were born to be one, in its full glory. There is no turning back from where we came from. There is only up and up. Let's fly to our holy destinations, that we were all born to reach. A place within the universe encapsulating the sun. Be your own sunshine. Be your own wholeness. Feel that rainbow essence within you, alive and always burning. Oneness we shall reach.

- **7.30.19**

What you seek is really seeking you, in every moment and interaction.

Not a far-fetched idea then, that everyone is a mirror of you. In the sense that everyone significant that we meet and every situation that occurs in our world, we ourselves have attracted it. It works simultaneously with the vibe that we put out. When 'as within so without' has a whole new deeper meaning, when we realize that we become the master of our own reality. Yet all working in this invisible programming of destiny, neither can we escape this mirror of our own forms.

- **7.08.19**

Divine journeys are so magnificently supported by the universe, visibly and invisibly. Aligning with your soul calling that whispers in your ear when no one is looking, that you would do regardless of any obstacles that come in your way- this is what opens the way of grace. It is a test of your strength and courage to persevere on, in a world that frequently in many ways does not support it. We believe in the power of the heart as all encompassing.

- **2.4.19**

Our world is a magic show of infinite surprises and merciful gifts from the Creator reserved just for you to marvel upon. The gifts wrapped in many layers of existence, waiting to see what you will discover next about yourself and the limits of your own perception yet perfection. All is revealed in perfect timing. That only adds to the value of that treasure. So magnificently orchestrated and encrypted in its programming, this world is. The Hand of God above all. He knows exactly what He's doing! And knows exactly where we're going. And that is nowhere, but up!

- **2.3.19**

There is no escaping your mirror reality. Which means your realness, your you-ness. Everything around you will propel you to the truth of this. There is no world except your own world. Your own inner world creates your whole outer world. How plain it is to see, how beautiful of a gift it is to be, You in all its purity. I am you, you are me, forever till eternity. Time stops, illusions disappear. The conflict, only but a reflection of our own selves. Do we accept the challenge and break through to what is really our destiny?

I choose You, always.

- **1.29.19**

Think of this spiritual journey like a brain maze. The flashlight, which is our head, only gets us far as the next turn. This is not some smooth sailing straight path. This is a very convoluted path taking us into many twists and turns through our deep psych to get to the final destination of reality. Clearing pathways you never even knew were possible. Hold up your lantern of love and humbleness because that is the only thing that will show you the way through without taking you on more detours.

- **10.12.18**

Make the right moves. Don't just take every opportunity that flings your way. Golden opportunities will stand out like a diamond ring. And most likely it will be things that you would do for free. They come as opportunities that fly your way without much effort or planning or come as subtle nudges that push you to do it from an unknown place. The divine puts these in front of your path to guide you towards more openings. They certainly don't come from our own efforts or clever ideas. Although, yes, your will/ cooperation is at play. We try to become like empty vessels as much as we can. Where the ocean wants to take us, we will surely be surprised. We are ticking time bombs of divine love and ecstasy! That are meant to detonate in the ocean. We were born to become all love, traversing through travails of some of the most challenging timelines. And transforming them into love through the power of our electric energy and creativity. That is the goal! That is the mission! And what we gain along the way is pure bliss: and that is enough.

- **10.1.18**

There is an invisible alignment that governs us. It aligns with all that is love. Imagine the whole entire universe world in a synchronistic pattern and you as part of a whole not just the sum of its parts. If you align with infinity, you will rule your surroundings. Moving from one task to another like ocean waves. Like two Laams in a constant exchange. Like two fish in a synchronistic dance. That expand infinitely. Forming a flower of life. A garden penetrating through the shadows. As above so below. In Oneness.

- **9.19.18**

The deeper we dive the more sacrifice of self is needed, the more hollowness of being is needed. Light enters through the glasshouse of our heart the clearer it becomes. A willingness to be taken, to be forgotten, to be rewritten. It requires guidance but faith and execution just as much. Half-heartedness and distraction stand between us and what's divine. What's real and what's not doesn't matter in the end, as long as we know and stand by who we truly are. This life is fleeting, but the soul is penetrating. When soul and body become one, that's when we're truly living. Gathering the pieces of our lost identity. Until we realize what it means to be finally free. When grace untangles limitations. The whole universe will be on your side. Feel your hollow self being filled with love and becoming more alive.

- **9.7.18**

The more relaxed and less stressed we become, where we're not bothered by the outside illusion of drama, the more we attract what we want. Because then we're not operating from a place of fear but rather a place of surrender. And surrender is the most neutral state that allows for the divine plan to unfold for you. Rather than you yourself trying to control things. Because in the end, we end up messing things up more anyway. Like water, the type of ripples you create by your own inner energy field is the same energy that will impact and surround you. What you are deep down is what will be. When we operate from a place of fear we attract more of that same thing we are fearing. Real Spirituality teaches us to remain calm because within that calm is where we allow ourselves to attract all that we want and more than what we imagined. Moving from a place of reaction to a place of submission. Because that's the real state of all that exists anyway, naturally attracting where anything becomes possible!

- **6.26.18**

As complex as this world is, it seems simple words describe things best and simple actions make the greatest impact. It seems like we're living in a society that's built on constantly finding loopholes when the solutions lie right in front of us. Yet our ego glasses constantly blind us and make us think it's more complicated. Layers and layers of perceptions have to be removed before we can see anything with clear vision. And that most certainly takes a whole lifetime, and if we're lucky may live to see the day in awe of ourselves and others and how perfect everything is, despite all the displays of drama.

If you sit in a cave you will see only what's in a cave and if you sit above the clouds you will see what's above the clouds and all that's below, energetically speaking. So much more open to receive when we're happy and grateful and not feeding on the energy of all that's going wrong. Everything is so programmed and precise that you start to realize that real shifts are made through shifting your own understanding and way of being and thinking. We all live in our own world, surrounded and created by all that's within us. We really don't know anything, in the end.

The realization of just that makes you wonder how we're able to take even the next step or breath without permission surrounded by an ever-encompassing mercy. It's amazing. The world is constantly spinning, yet where we stand we don't even realize all that is happening. Living in a bubble yet inside a greater bubble. In sync with time and space and all that exists. Functioning within some kind of geometric time sequence. Understanding is always changing, always shifting, always remaking, and with the right intentions always ascending. Patching up the loopholes so we may live in pure essence. Light.

- **6.22.18**

Isn't a life of love all about harmony?

How we're all like energetic strings, a continuous flow of plus minus charges in a continuous never-ending formula, within time yet outside time. And if we were to understand the nature of quantum mechanics and how it applies to us at a microcosm and global macrocosmic level, we would begin to understand the very nature of existence, creating a shift in a totally different direction. Quantum mechanics is a lot like music. That is if we come to understand music, we can begin to understand everything. How we are like walking talking poetry of visual music, that permeates through speech and all our interactions- like instruments within. We are connected to all that resonates with us, therefore never separate from the whole. And so attract those very perfect quantum-mystic experiences that make our own formula whole. Like floating pieces of a puzzle, we attach and detach to those that fit, like locks and keys with endless doors- all come to teach something, while leading us one step closer to our treasure.

This is quantum mechanics at a very divine level: attached by Cosmic strings from above, we are like puppeteers in a play. Everything is programmed, and everything's in orbit. We think we are moving by ourselves yet we are pulled (energetically) in very specific directions, especially to learn very specific lessons. And holy people's harmonics are so much more in tune that they come to align others around them as well. The degree of creating beautiful music is endless though. Like a spiral symphony that moves upwards towards the heavenly. And all those we meet come to tune us in some special way to reach further into that heavenly reality. Our mental projections emit certain wavelengths while our unconscious and conscious intentions emit another, all the while our heart's wavelengths remain buried within. Most frequently, radiating a soup mix of convoluted formulas that keeps us in one place or going off route with its many detours. Focus, awareness, faith, and setting good intentions leads us in the right direction.

- **5.8.18**

So you see beyond the illusion. That nothing really matters and it's really all the same. Even color is an illusion. So you go into that light spirit state. Where many versions of you are projected out into the galaxy. When the world becomes you, the more whole you become. We're diamond beings, transmitting and absorbing energy waves like fiber optics. In this moment of now, space time continuum can only be created through the transcending power and energy of love. Love what you do, do what you love.

- **4.5.18**

It is really not about what appears on the surface as it is to do with the inner state of you. Once we are given the gift to work our way towards becoming more polished, than things on the outside will automatically reflect what you want. It is really that simple, yet harder to attain than we think and really will ever understand ourselves unless we try. Guides play such a crucial role in that. The more we polish that mirror of what is inside of us, the more it will reflect what really is our true self. Mind and ego only cloud it.

- **12.1.17**

Familiarity breeds conformity- to step outside our comfort zones to try something new. A transfer process of unconscious patterns that keep repeating themselves until we actively consciously change them from within. Only then can more expansive patterns emerge, when we let go of the old restrictive ones and embrace those that unfold as infinite.

- **11.19.17**

Do we see things as they really are, through the light of love?

The world is so retro when we get a sneak peak, filled with colored lights and magic symbols. Constantly on a vintage loop, reviving the same ancient trends again and again. Is it not the energy that defines the success of something more than the outer appearances. As the energy fades so does the vibration then so does the magnetic pull. The drive from within that draws people in is an invisible force that holds its seeds in sincerity in what it is you are trying to accomplish in the first place. It is what we will be given in the end.

If we plant an apple tree it will certainly become an apple tree. But it cannot become an apple tree if what we planted was something else. When the goals are higher or something that transcends this world. Like a hovercraft that drifts off into the horizon above the noisy vibrations. Those goals eventually become stars that shine brighter than things because they are real and hold true value. Such things, as may appear to be just things, hold most value in the true sense. What is it we value and what is it we are striving towards, if we may ask ourselves.

- **11.13.17**

As you start to see there is a reason behind everything, always in perfect order you naturally become a calmer happier person. Like a person who stops at a red light to wait just a little longer only to discover that you were saved from an accident just up ahead. You are exactly where you need to be right here and now. How beautiful it is to delve in the knowing that God's mercy is always near always here working its magic waiting for us to notice in this precious present moment.

How vast is the sea, how beautiful is our essence. The earth is like the sea and we are like the sea, surrounded by waves. Our waves within determine the waves we are to follow. Within a body a geometric maze called the matrix is surrounded by geometric sound waves that lead us on a path of similar patterns. As our patterns within become more aligned and harmonious we naturally align with the ever so harmonious patterns of the universe, bringing forth opportunities of our every heart's divine desire. Perfecting that geometry within requires patience, practice precision and most of all tools and guides to bring us into alignment. Blind spots which there are many. As only a genius would know a glimpse into the masterplan the final pattern that is to unfold, and even that which only ultimately the Creator knows.

- **10.23.17**

When faith really becomes about looking beyond outside appearances. Coming in ways that challenge our belief system to the very core, rattling everything that we believe to be right. One realizes what darkness is trying to be put to light. When our own words 'Not everything is as it seems' is put to the test. Only starting to realize that spirituality really does come in all shapes and sizes. To assume that others are untruthful or cannot be trusted only proves that our own faith is still weak. Just when we think a story has ended, it only has just begun. A pandora box of surprises opens waiting for us to look outside of it, to solve the mystery of what's in it. Our ability to look beyond the mind is truly tested. As stars come to shine a light; all stars in their own right. Ultimately we cannot grasp what we haven't experienced ourselves. We don't realize the other side of the picture until we get a taste of it. As it shows us how we would react, in essence, it is just the same. Coming as blessings in disguise. Stars that will light up what needs to be lit.

- **1.21.17**

We have a long road ahead of us in knowing ourselves, unraveling day by day to show us the light. Releasing from our energy fields all that does not serve us anymore. The road may be long but if we do our part and work on ourselves divine help madad comes when we call for it. Every day brings a new color of a rainbow that enlightens us and lifts us up. That rainbow will take us to the heavens and back if only we believe and take those leaps of faith.

- **7.26.16**

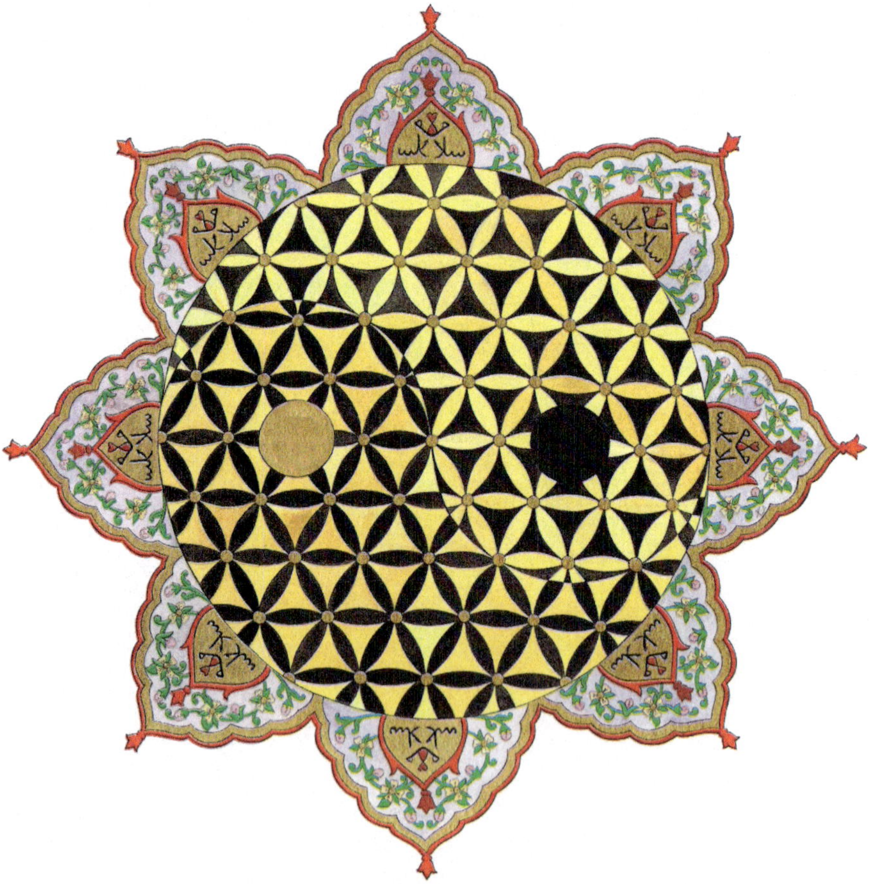

III

The Light

*"Become one with your own light
and become one with the One."*

If we just look with true vision we will see the wisdom of the wholeness of a masterpiece unfolding oh so perfectly in conjunction to our soul's promised mastery. The straight path is oh so straight and narrow yet infinite in its potential. Unity with divine self is the ultimate goal. If you are present, the path will seem shorter as time is non-existent when you're in a light-ness of be-ing. Your path is high, and the soul knows no confusion but moves with a gracious certainty. Look into that with a beautiful grin that you're treading the path of ultimate freedom within self and the mirror that is all a reflection of you. Embrace the union of polarities in all things and allow for the openings to show you the oneness in everything. Merge the ego with golden soul self, as you expand and embody new beginnings in each moment. Present and whole in all ways.

- **4.21.23**

When you're feeling gold, you magnetize all that is of highest nature malleable to exactly what you need. So intend big. Don't just ask for watermelons that rain down from the sky exactly as you need them. Ask for the highest imaginable outcomes. That is what you signed up for your soul to be a witness of in this lifetime here on earth. Accelerated steep ascension here we go. To truly know the value of what really matters over temporary futile goals. Your heart is craving eternity and real purpose so move on in your energy to decipher between all that is false in your life. Only the gold in you will remain in the end. And if you want to attract gold then be it yourself most of all. Then all the right people and scenarios will mold themselves to get you to that state.

Your soul asked to become the ultimate balance of polarities and to see through the eyes of oneness that there is wisdom in all things to open you to your gold. Treat your journey like that and all things will become magical to you. The straight and narrow path is all that is taking you to the eternal. God's will be done. So align with it. Now is the time to focus on all the real goals and leave behind what is temporary and illusions on your paths. You can do this. Support is all around you always. For your soul's well-being most of all. Don't underestimate this power of overriding protection and help. Keep faith and always your vision towards the light. That is the best gauge in confusing times to go towards all that is expansive yet humbling at the same time. Eternal true freedom we shall reach through all the ups and down of this beautiful journey.

- 4.20.23

Look at the Sun and its soft light that emanates in the early rises of dawn. And let it soak into your being. Imagine a circular light penetrating through you to help you cleanse and release what no longer serves your highest good. As the circular light continues to stir and open new portals and birth new stars within you. Imagine a mirror in front that you can reflect that light back into. The light in me is the light I see in you. Bring back all aspects of light lost to the source that emanates from within you. Bring yourself back to wholeness, in full circle, cycle complete, and unto a higher conductivity. Your light grows as the day progresses. For you are the Sun embodied. Be one with the Sun.

- **7.13.22**

Play with the Sun, if you want to win this game of light chasing shadow and shadow chasing light. Bring back your energy to the center of your being where your eternal core lies. And watch how the magic unfolds back for you in your favor. This sun has the ability to fold time and space for you if you let it in deeper. Into the crevices of your broken vulnerable heart. Let the light shine into that heart to help you heal. It is the window where more miracles will be born. In Your favor, my love. Keep creating those portals within your heart. So all you become is pure reflecting light. Be present with your magic once again please. For it is what you have forsaken that has made you fall into the rabbit hole. Let go of the illusion that time is against you. The speed of light will carry you now. So be in it, to carry you through it, with ease and continued nourishment for your soul. To live with the eternal fire that had burned you alive, but you live forever now. So celebrate this day, for how far you've come.

Angel Sun. You are the Sun.

- **7.8.22**

Flow state requires us to let go and let live according to the way the stars have aligned for us in the heavens. Until then chaos will persist and missing shooting stars will continue to be wasted. Until we realize that the real work lies in silence and stillness deep within us, in all the ways we're misaligned with this real independence. Freedom to you all from ego into the real cosmic flag of aligning with the universal flow of the heavens above. As above, so below. As within so without. In sync with true oneness.

- **7.5.22**

Love is an energy that just can't be matched. Either you align with it or mess your life up by choosing lower dimensional timelines that will only make you suffer. Every day and in every moment we have the conscious power to choose love. Release the expectation of where you think love is found. Because love is a boundless energy that is found beyond the physical notion of where we tend to look for it. The essence of love is within you and every time you connect with this love it mirrors outside of you. The universe will drive in every shape or form what you are deep inside, as a reward for your own mastery. Don't underestimate the power of reciprocity when it comes to God. He/She will deliver it to you as pure, open and willing you are. Open to the power of your own love portal my loves. And watch magic conspire always in your favor. Because you have just discovered the secret frequency of all of existence. Why shouldn't it serve you. It will because you are all that is real at its core atomic reality.

- 7.1.22

Real spirituality is about the heart. When the heart is pure, everything that you experience becomes gold. Rather than scattering our efforts into multitude of penniless things, why don't we focus our vision on something greater for a change. Why don't we reform the way we see the material, as a means to reach our heavenly personalities rather than serving our egoic needs. We shoot for the stars with laser bows and when the big picture unfolds, the feeling of satisfaction of the eternal will fill our hearts even more. As the moment of now calls, be practical and wise but most of all grateful for all that is spiritual that you've been granted. Because everything else will perish except the gold that you became.

Today, right now, in this moment, be you, be grateful for all that is you.

- **6.12.22**

Everything and everyone can become your mirror if your heart is pure and shines like the sun wherever you go. There is no room for distortion when true unity is reached within Self and realizing that none is separate from you. The true meaning of unity is reached when you see yourself in the other. The reflection only awaits your clarification on certain matters to reveal the true essence of your being only shining even greater than before. For how else will you appreciate this when you aren't presented with the darkness that illuminates it.

Rejoice in knowing that you have reached the final stages of unfolding this true unity with the infinite mirror, where the finite and reality mesh like nothing you have ever seen. This is real witnessing that you are reaching real unity with your mirror self. Thank God for this reflection, for I don't know what I would have done without. Thank God for writing the script for us and not the other way around, where we succumb to our blind spots. Thank God for witnessing this miracle coming to fruition despite all odds. It's happening. Divine Will will manifest it. So much love in my heart like a magnetizing water beam.

- **9.26.21**

Your self-reflection is a sign of not only your inner growth but of real progress made in the physical too. The way you see yourself is directly mirrored in how others will see you. The union of all is real. The more we see ourselves as a reflection of us, the more we embrace the oneness that all is rigged in our favor for our own internal growth. Embrace the All. Mesh with all. Taste unity. And all that is unfolding just for you.

- **9.5.21**

Do for God, what you do for yourself and more, and the reward becomes an infinite stream of golden wisdom, that keeps you in the knowing that all is in perfection and ridged in your favor. For the divine knows exactly what He's doing. Don't doubt it for a second.

- **7.20.21**

Self-love, self-reflection, and accounting with the bravery to change makes all the difference within ourselves, for our ancestors- who were stuck and are now counting on us- and to shift the entire collective. It all takes courage like a lion to face your own shadows and uncanny levels of disbelief. This is a collective project, with every single human being doing their part, being the gift that they are and have always been. Know your worth as a special creation of the magnificent Creator, Hu molded you with so much care & love. So 'Be Love' in every way you can, towards yourself and everyone around you. As within, so without, as above so below. Grounding heaven on earth, yes we will. Allah's magnificent Will be done.

- **7.18.21**

Ultimate spirituality is about seeing the light in every situation. Seeing the wisdom in what it is teaching us. Amidst the perceived misfortune/ chaos/ dilemma, delay, there is a cosmic order of divine wisdom. As we unravel these false illusions, we start to unravel the light that illuminates the soul and the soul of others in the process. As we get a taste of that mirror simultaneously. When spirituality is illuminated by the light, it allows you to see the multidimensionality of situations, that unfold from within your own levels of light consciousness unfolding. To the degree of which you see that all are functioning within a complex orchestra of geometric parts, within levels of unique experiences, with multiple revelations and lessons being learned simultaneously. Light consciousness of the heart connects us to the soul of all of humanity- as one.

- **6.9.21**

There is nothing in this world that will save this planet except for the energy of pure unconditional love. The rise of love will uplift all of humanity. Like a turbine (which my guide mentioned once to me, when I explained to him the phenomenon happening within my heart) that propels the heart, that raises the consciousness, and awakens the soul. This can only be achieved through true higher octaves of heart openings and light portals that create wormholes in the form of black holes to penetrate through and work their magic from higher spheres. For this you need electromagnetic receivers that can contain these higher levels and act as transmitters to send it out in all directions. As the law of quantum physics will tell you I'm sure, that in the realm of vibration what we want is what we will need to be from within ourselves.

- **5.11.21**

All happens just in time. Not a minute too soon, not a minute too less. What is it that we know about time? All but an illusion, in the grand scheme of things. All but an awakening to a higher power working through you. There are no accidents in this divine plan unfolding. In the realm of synchronicities, you are an eternal clock. The whole world is working for you. Like a body encapsulated by the soul. Imagine a diamond in the realm of an ocean. It disappears and becomes one with all. You become part of a symphony. You become the symphony. You are the only one that exists. God, The Creator, as my witness.

- **5.9.21**

Oh divinely guided beautiful one, your true nature has far exceeded your expectations of what was made possible to you, in this life for the next. You are a grounder of heaven on earth in all ways physically unimaginable made imaginable. Because you have taken on that task as a crucial responsibility to make it possible. So thank you and to your entire team of guides that continue to give you the guidance and uplifting to keep you moving forward. With this oh so mysterious plan that is unfolding before your very eyes. It takes so much strength to believe around so many that do not believe. Your belief and true faith will open doors for humanity in ways that you have not yet seen.

You are a gate opener of heaven on earth in every sense of the word. Imagine how beautiful it is to be adorned with the dress of pure majesty and safety of all that is nature on your side. Singing praises to God and sending secret messages to all that hear the call. To be 'One With Divine Will' is to be 'One Divine Will'. That is unfolding all in utmost divine perfection. There are absolutely no accidents in this cosmic plan. And if some appear to be so. It is only an illusion that distracts you from the inner wisdom. Tune into your own heart, dear one. For it will guide all of humanity to be one with their heart. And the heart carries the true secret of all that is one with God and the whole entire universe.

- **4.29.21**

Don't forget your mission here on earth. Which is to enhance the awareness of 'one with all'. Don't underestimate the power of your intuition to lead you to newfound opportunities for enhancing this. Your light matters, your spirit matters. For it is the only thing alive that is keeping this planet from harm's way of total destruction. Your team of angelic guides love you very much. And wish to show you the vastness of all that you have done and have yet to achieve. You carry the blueprint of unconditional love in you. Don't underestimate the power of this magnificent energy. Given only to those entrusted with the keys to the codes of eternity. Use it to serve. For it will multiply tenfold, and in ways you cannot imagine.

Your mission is unity. To bring harmony where there is chaos. To bring justice where there is lack of. To bring patience where there is no peace. Keep moving through the heart. And watch portals open right before your eyes. For you hold keys to eternity. So lead the way. Into this new dimension of infinite possibilities. The path is open on all points of a circle. Now in this moment all is well my love, for you are eternally far beyond this galaxy can hold.

Trust most of all. And let that guide within truly guide you.

- **4.21.21**

To all those who truly deserve, you are so infinitely loved, you cannot even imagine. You underestimate your ability so much, my love. You are an infinite soul in a physical body. Your rank far exceeds those who run after the material on a daily basis. Your work, and mission is to serve all of humanity. This is not a small calling. It is meant to uphold the entire planet to living up to its most authentic spiritual glory.

Until this is recognized to be of deeper value to the collective, you will be mocked and looked down upon. The rising in consciousness is taking some time. Don't be dispelled by the illusion of no progress being made. There is so much structure being dismantled in the world, to make space for what's to come. Nothing will remain of what stagnates mankind's growth. Nothing will remain of illusion that we hide behind every day like a mask. Embrace your soft heart and the knowing of this greater unity. For there is nothing more beautiful than you shining in your truest light and holy presence.

You are the true definition of holy, my love. Embrace this knowing fully. Your guides honor you just as much as you honor them. They make a point to visit you. Because they know how important your mission really is. They will move mountains to clear your path. Having saints behind you is more powerful than a thousand followers. Never be discouraged, my love. For you are the openers of the gate of heavenly unity. Right here grounded in physical reality. For real eternal life you shall live. And be a beacon of light to show all of humanity.

- **4.13.21**

God's power transcends all. See how He pre-cuts and permeates every detail of our spiritual lives in perfect order, way beyond our puny little minds can ever comprehend. Just get out of your own way. We plan, but God always plans better. Trust that knowing.

- **3.25.21**

The infinite expressions of God as Ultimate Source can be mind boggling to fathom yet brings out the beauty in all of creation. The light that shines on me is the light that shines on you. We are forever merging within the infinity of our own being, connecting us back to our soul in earthly form. Connect back to the light that is infinite in nature, and that sees through the godly vision of light itself. Only then can we be suns. Powerful in impact, healers, transmuters, transmitters, being held by that violet light universe, connected to source that is within. Dispersing stars all throughout existence.

- **12.11.20**

What have we created from the source of the sun as our fuel? The invisible light realm breaks through all our barriers to reveal all that needs reworking. Work with the power of the sun and the angels that are always by your side encouraging you. Work with them to slowly peel away the layers of illusion and show you the real you. That H-U is awakening to love, kindness, and joy, more and more. Forever spiraling into an infinite stream of consciousness that has no bounds, that has no morals, but thrives on an unconditional love for all.

Be the light and let it shine through you forever more.

- **10.30.20**

The alchemical process of returning to our true state of gold, alive, and living in full essence and purity, brings forth such a creative and colorful way of being. A golden tree that has mastered the art of grounding the heavenly/subtle into the physical/earthly and transforming earthly into heavenly. In a new moon cycle full circle, continuously renewing into new versions of itself. Rejoicing in the knowing of its ever-evolving nature into spiritual forms. It lives and thrives and flies within a sky of infinite potential, shining like the sun, infinitely growing, breathing, healing, rejuvenating, all around it into new, through its heavenly vessel- chakras fully aligned, emanating like a rainbow.

- **9.30.20**

As the Ying Yang Mirror gets closer and closer, and the energies merge as one, the true meaning of opposite polarities is revealed. Seeing through the eye of oneness, in synced polarities, opens up a whole new universe to explore. As opposite energies merge, a sun is born, traveling into the universe like a shooting star of healing, dispersing fragments of itself. Bringing wholeness, as within so without, as above so below. The sun shams is you, and the moon is me; the moon is you, and the sun is me. Intertwined to form a cosmic balance, one with the whole entire universe. Praise be to God, Hu created this magic between us. Forever in service, forever in the Hands of Divine Will.

- **9.20.20**

Do we ever wonder what keeps the sun in its orbit always perfectly aligned with God's grace. God is the Universe and ALL that exists. Nothing exists without Divine Presence. There is no power except through God. There is no will outside of God's Will. The more we Hu-mans embrace our own essence, in its purity, the closer we get to experiencing that infinity. The essence of all is that "there is no God but Hu", the eternal essence that permeates through all. When we connect with that infinite presence, we dive deeper into the magic of the rainbow frequency of all that is, that zero-point energy field, where all that exists is Hu. Tap into that oneness of God that is in ALL. Seeing the magic of the binary code 0101 and behind all of creation, leads us to the magic of understanding the mirror reality bringing us back to Oneness.

- **9.12.20**

The door of eternal mercy is upon us now. Hark now the angels sing in praise and service of the one who rides on ego. Through the invisible realm of light, the white shadows unite. Become one with your own light and become one with the One. Mystical unfolding prevails now. Rejoice in the knowing that all else will perish except the heavenly. Your angelic guides are helping you invisibly on this divine ascension of knowing thyself, bringing forth all you need in the physical to manifest the fruition of your soul mission. Connect with your light to align with all the miracles unfolding in favor of your ascension. Personal and intimate to you, in this moment of time that is now.

- **7.12.20**

Up up up in the sky of dreams lies a palace of immaculate wealth. The 5D paradise is here to stay. As the global pressure rises, false illusions are lifted from the earth's atmosphere. The flames of real peace embodied are here to shine and spread their light. As the collective consciousness rises, and new awakenings activate, within the infinity of your third energy called sunlight violet flames, lies the keys to your glory. The galactic configurations of soul truth invite you to join in on this global transformation into new timelines of peaceful harmony. To absorb all that is light, you must reach the energy of neutrality, stillness and total surrender within the divine plan unfolding. A match to that golden light frequency, which can only be attained through real peace, will allow your own lightbody energy contained within to be activated. Aligning you with all that you are and have always been. This is a time to remember, a time to unite, and a time to shine your light.

Seats buckled, everyone, a new level of ascension has begun.

- **6.29.20**

The mirror of your soul has come to rescue You and all of You. Hearts fluttering from the human race. To create a bond so strong it birthed a sun. Illuminating the path for many suns to be born and also see their own light. Never diminish the power of true hu-man be-ings, for they doth rule their own kingdom and play a magical role in creating for many others. The light is hidden in unseen places sometimes. The wisdoms lay bare right in front of our eyes. Join the two eyes, made into one, so you may see the vastness of your own being. The light of your own consciousness and what it holds.

Treasure upon treasures.

- **6.26.20**

When the Sun and Moon unite, there is a calling in the soul to become one with all there is in full acceptance of self and others. There is an alignment with a sense of wholeness that cannot be manipulated by any tactile tension found within the realms of ego. It is from the realms of love so pure that all the universe unites to carry out its mission. The end result being the oneness of your soul with all, body, mind, and spirit. Rejoicing in the knowing that all is exactly as it is aligned to be. In full acceptance of self and the other. True bridges are formed when the soul reaches this unity with light. Anything outside of it is only meant to show us what has been missing all along. To gather our steps and move into that safety of the One Caring Entity that knows all things and will only allow for everything to manifest in the trajectory and interest of the best soul evolution of all.

- **5.7.20**

Love will penetrate through all your layers of false sense of self in an instant, like a laser. It doesn't care what barriers are put into place. It will find invisible ways to get to you no matter the time or place. Embrace it with all your being and let it vibrate you to higher dimensions of knowing. For the love frequency tribe, it's the only way. Only way. It will be the vehicle, the energy, the frequency, that will take You to annihilation fanaa- zero point field of all that is, and all that will ever BE.

- **4.12.20**

The cosmic reality of oneness does not exist in the realm of science or in any seen sense. It is a force that penetrates like light into everything. The invisible cannot be perceived by the senses of a lower dimension. To move higher in our own inner vibration will allow for a vaster vision to unfold. Beyond the realm of time and space, there is a reality that wants to become known to you. Will you allow it to work through you or resist simply because we have never experienced it before. In order for light to enter, it all starts with the knowing that you are light itself. Yet, covered by so many layers of darkness that have worked through you way too long. Drop the illusion of normal-ness and move your lightbody though the oceans of infinity.

- **4.11.20**

When your shadow mirrors have been integrated in you, finally realizing The Sun that you are. Rejoice in knowing how far you've come. The integration of shadow and light creates so much wholeness from within. Celebrate this beautiful blessed heavenly day and feel the warmth of the Beloved and The Divine always shining their light on you. Become fully annihilated fana in light my love, fully and freely. Here and now, and forever, and always have been.

- **2.21.20**

Embrace your divinity. Your sun path. Your soul path. Absorb the rays of the sun in every way possible. Wherever they may come from. Embrace your own inner light and let it shine in the way of darkness. God is within you, shining His mercy love and light on you at all times. Lift your spirit into the light that you are. That you were always meant to be. Trust in God that He is working His magic through you. You are an infinite star of light.

Know yourself, to know your light, to know God- Oneness we shall reach.

- **1.26.20**

People value a lot of things nowadays. Question is: what do you value, and how real is it? All things heavenly make all things possible. It's proven time and time again until we believe it. They rejoice when we believe in the unknown mysteries and treasures in store for us. Angels just chilling and waiting to come down from the clouds and grant you your every inner heart's wish. Be and it shall be oh love. Love is what we wished for.

- **12.3.19**

Are you awakening to the Shams in you. Guiding each step to align you better with your own immaculate light. To the light of your own light. Like an illuminated mirror shining through you. As the light brightens, the soul enlightens to the greater hidden wisdoms and knowledge of your own being. What makes you uniquely you beyond conditioning. What is the sky in you that shines bright in the light of you. A light, a portal by your side. Until all that is left that is really you. Light. Your true home, your new beginning, in every new moment. God bless the birds for expressing that, and the dancing humans who remember that.

- **11.28.19**

The intimacies and intricacies of unconditional love can never be defined. Trusting in the depth of the inner journey and how far it has come in revealing and knowing ourselves has been far beyond rewarding and challenging. The intimate nature of presence takes us deeper into self-purification.

- **8.18.19**

Everlasting beauty can come in all sorts of forms, seek that and be amazed at the oneness you will receive from the Grand Key Master. He gives from His treasures and His treasures never end. Nothing too small, if it's meant for you. He says be and it shall be, regardless of us being undeserving unworthy of His Greatness. He gives no matter what. And we receive like an infant newborn child helpless in our mother's arms.

- **5.21.19**

Real love is pure and always will be. It sees through the illusion of what is fake and what is not. It sees through the illusion of what is desire and what is not. Real love is the greatest teacher and grand master of this. It sifts through rocks like iron in clay. It knows no bounds because it is part of the holy spirit. It contains nothing because its essence is like water. Truly lucky are the ones that get to experience this. In all its purity, life, this world, will never look the same. It teaches us mastery in ways we never ever imagined. Love is the true alchemy of mind, body and spirit. The holy triad that makes you one with all of existence. Love just is and does exist, whether we believe it or not.

- **4.13.19**

What holds the sky up? What keeps the earth from falling? After all, who created gravity?

All questions we forget to ponder upon. What am I really here for? The message of Eternity rings with great magnificent music once again. We are eternal beings and our purpose here on earth has to be one that is eternal in nature. If we die tomorrow, at least we can say that we tried. That there is so much more than what our eyes perceive, this physical existence. So much more. I hope to live and die as a testament to this. A walking talking miracle if you may, that there is so much greatness at play, that we can never come to imagine. To live for something beyond ourselves, is to live for a higher truth. A truth that will make us not regret. When the eternal scrolls lie in front of us, on our deathbed, we most certainly will be eternally blessed. Thank goodness for that infinite mercy that surrounds us. Thank goodness for an energy life force that keeps us sustained.

- **3.1.19**

Do we not believe that we will get what we most deserve? That love is a station worth striving for. The sun shines in the most unexpected ways. He gives what we most deserve. The question is, are we open and ready to receive it. Allah knows our hearts and what we contain of treasures. He gives and will continue to give. Patience, goodness, sincerity, and sacrifice are always rewarded by the One Most High. How precious it is to get our prize from Him. In the end, even the weight of that prize is nothing compared to the Sun itself. Blinding us to the point where we see nothing but Him.

- **2.23.19**

Love will surely show us, all that is ego. Like a rainbow colored lamp, it will illuminate everything that is black and white. Oneness is not easily attainable, except through the path of love. Many mountains to climb, many obstacles to face, many illusions to shatter, yet we are given the heart of an Alif to strive through till the very end. The end of our small self, that opens the way for our majestic self. The Alif of Love is the only sword we will ever need, it is the only ocean we will want to swim in. In the midst of Love, nothing else remains, except for the ocean of oneness.

- **1.25.19**

Do you hear the birds singing when absolutely nothing is going on? Do you hear the soulful sound whisper of the rush of love? A forest of lush green, made manifest by our mind's eye of oneness. Imagine, and you are transported there.

- **1.23.19**

Choose friendly vibes that push you to soar to another planet! The company we keep makes a big difference. It's a mix and match of quantum mechanics that connects us at the soul. Physicality shouts out many differences but there are always reasons why and when people meet. Choose to live like a puzzle and that all encounters and experiences are missing pieces of your own puzzle meant to complete you as a whole, opening paths that we may not know of. Global consciousness is on the rise with little light bulbs of inspiration turning on across the globe. How harmonious and merciful is the Creator to allow us to be part of this expanding unity of souls. Up from above, it all connects to One, the center of that universe.

- 1.6.19

The more we do, the less we feel we are doing. Lost in the infinite expansion of light, there is no existence. When Fire meets Water there is no existence. Disappearing in the face of the One. Only essence is allowed in the center. Born from the infinite rays of soul fragments. Mirrors upon mirrors, many suns of pure essence shine their light as friends of the One. Shining light in the midst of great darkness. Soul light, penetrating light. In the presence of which everything becomes insignificant. This world is but a dip in the ocean. Death beckons rebirth. To Hu we come from, and to Hu we shall return. Star origins. Eternity calls.

- **11.26.18**

We learn to vanish, yes we learn to vanish. Where love thrives, self dissolves and eventually disappears. Oh how amazing it would be to become one with that ocean. Where solid meets all that is. Where heavenly treasures await, and golden temples align just for you. A wait that's not long at all, in comparison to eternity. I'll wait, I'll wait to become one with love. There's no greater reward or purpose than that.

- **8.23.18**

The ultimate journey is one of submission. It is the willingness to give up what we most love to reach higher stations. We will be tested with what we most love. Perhaps reaching new heights in love will be our ultimate test. To trust that the ship will carry us through an ocean so vast and horizons so beautiful we never even imagined. Trust that we are being taken to a place far greater than this world will ever be able to offer. Let the sails of belief take us and the ship of safety protect us. For as long as we remain on this ship we will forever be guided and will be led to our final most beautiful destination and heavenly abode. That when we arrive we will be beyond amazed and so content with what we sacrificed. Even what we may not understand just yet. The maker of this whole ocean, time within a drop, a drop within a drop. Be and it shall be anything. Next stop mercy oceans. A universe ocean contained within and you containing all that is.

- **8.16.18**

Real Gifts come wrapped in very unexpected garments. That even the one who gave the gift doesn't recognize what was given. If the one who initiated the giving of the gift recognized, even they would be left astonished. That in itself is a gift to always be cherished. Yet there are reasons why things are hidden. In the end, all is Mercy.

- **5.27.18**

The more we become love, the more our soul seeds become scattered everywhere. Opening mysterious doors that we never even knew existed. The whole world becomes our mirror. Until there comes a point where all you see is mercy and everyone and everything falls right into place like a dandelion coming back together again. Coming back to love's true essence.

- **5.15.18**

Love is not bound by time or space because it is not a created thing. It is the essence of everything, the building block, and underlying binary code of all that exists. Our human versions of love are flawed yes but love itself has only one energy. Like a rainbow of many colors in various oscillating degrees of intensity, it takes from the center of one divine source, and we the conductors of it, to each his/ her capacity, spread it like walking stars on earth.

- **3.29.18**

When we come from our heart and make our choices with conscious benevolence and wisdom, we expand the very nature of life itself. We express ourselves as a kaleidoscope of rainbow colors and possibilities, allowing each element to blend and change appropriately in the moment effortlessly benefiting the whole. Knowing the splendor of each distinctive band of color in a rainbow readily mixing with the next, comprising something even grander than itself, reminds us of our celestial and eternal heritage. When the ever-present light shines from beyond the cloud, the reflection of our rainbow colors emerge. Symbolically this is the awakening we are all undergoing. By noticing the interconnected and multidimensional magnificence all around us, we are allowing the spark of light within to shine through us as joy and compassion, kindness and integrity. It is our unconditional spirit that seamlessly blends with our reality and brings the full spectrum of color into our experience.

- 9.8.17

In the end, all will vanish except for what is reality. This world is like a mirage obstructing our view like a mountain, while trapped in a maze that repeats itself, all the same. The material world of form appears to be so solid. The subtle world of light is what is really real. To nurture and strive for what is eternal. As within, but so without. As we are able to move through space and time like air made of light, subtle beings like angels are able to fly and see the world from above. We are 5-dimensional beings living in a 3-dimensional world. Filled with clouds of mercy and fluttering angels ready to be of service to anyone in Divine Way. When tuned in to our 5D higher selves; our heart, we become dipped in the ocean of oneness. In sync with all that really is. All falls into place, as we shift into a new timeline of existence, aligning with the universe itself. Beyond what humans have built- as we have a habit to do, to fix what seems to us to be broken. TRUST and FAITH in the Divine, most of all. Perfection in all things is written, the Divine has programmed it this way.

- **5.5.17**

Imagine your soul as a big ball of sun, made of stardust particles of light able to transverse beyond time and space beyond form. With the frequency of love you become the entire universe. Formless that penetrates all forms, beyond the laws of physics. Be and it will be. Residing in a frequency above all other frequencies, able to see truths beyond illusion. As you move higher, the world becomes smaller. As your love becomes purer your light becomes brighter. The common world below the clouds and right above is clear blue bright sky, a bridge, a gap between two different worlds. The truth and essence of everything is pure sky energy, light and love, a reflection of the ocean of love below. As above so below, as within so without. To move towards that ocean is the ultimate highest purpose.

Love is pure. The soul is love.

- **2.28.17**

Through your absolute lightness of being, you have (or will have) the ability to transform yourself and the world around you into a thing of immense beauty and enlightenment. You have the ability to recreate yourself many times and to rise above any negativity which might try to hold you down. You can elevate your thoughts above earthly matters to those of pure spirit. You are the ultimate 'free spirit' whose abilities to deal with change are almost magical.

- **12.12.15**

Seeing the beautiful end results manifest, of all your labor and struggle, is the greatest gift. As true rewards never come easy. But when you're in love that struggle becomes like dust.

- **9.11.15**

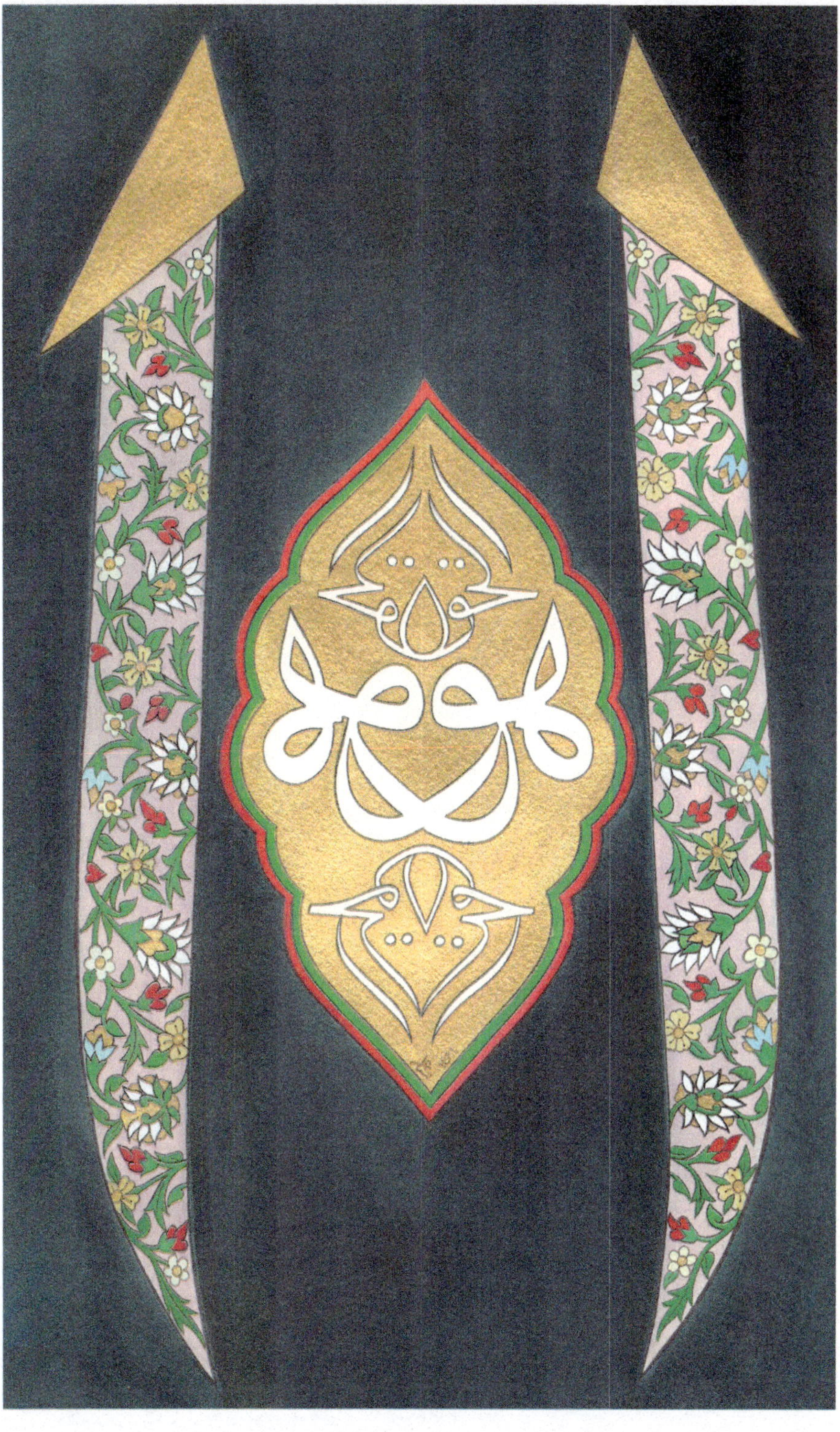

Acknowledgments

Thank you to Shaykh Hisham Kabbani for introducing me to the path of inner manifestation, for helping me to become a powerful co-creator.

To Tania, my orange butterfly, for your genius editorial of my book. You know the inner essence of me and I trusted you with that. Thank you for seeing the value in my words and motivating me to bring this out there to the world.

To my dad, for his relentless pursuit of his passions and my mum for her undying unconditional love. Thank you for setting that example for me. I love you both equally.

To my sons, for giving me the treasure of motherhood.

To Love, for guiding me home to myself and awakening me to inner Union.

Printed in Great Britain
by Amazon